Wicked
NORTHERN ILLINOIS

A photograph of Starved Rock, taken in the early 1900s, showing its location on the Illinois River. The site was the scene of legendary bloodshed during the 1700s and went on to become a place of horror after a triple murder galvanized Northern Illinois in 1960.

Wicked
NORTHERN ILLINOIS

THE DARK SIDE OF
THE PRAIRIE STATE

TROY TAYLOR

THE
History
PRESS

Published by The History Press
Charleston, SC 29403
www.historypress.net

Copyright © 2010 by Troy Taylor
All rights reserved

First published 2010

Manufactured in the United States

ISBN 978.1.59629.278.9

Library of Congress Cataloging-in-Publication Data

Taylor, Troy.
Wicked northern Illinois : the dark side of the Prairie State / Troy Taylor.
p. cm.
Includes bibliographical references.
ISBN 978-1-59629-278-9
1. Violent crimes--Illinois--History--Anecdotes. 2. Murder--Illinois--History--Anecdotes.
3. Crime--Illinois--History--Anecdotes. 4. Criminals--Illinois--Biography--Anecdotes.
5. Victims of crimes--Illinois--Biography--Anecdotes. 6. Illinois--History--Anecdotes. 7.
Illinois--Biography--Anecdotes. 8. Illinois--Social conditions--Anecdotes. I. Title.
HV6793.I3T395 2010
364.109773'2--dc22
2010031975

Contents

Acknowledgements

I would like to thank the many other writers and chroniclers of Illinois history and crime who came before me, especially Herbert Asbury, Jay Robert Nash, Paul Angle, Randall Parrish, Milo Quaife and Stu Fliege. I'd also like to thank my friend John Winterbauer for his continued assistance with all things dark and my editor at The History Press, Ben Gibson, who put up with my many quirks and oddities. And finally, thanks to my wife, Haven, for her continued patience and love and for really getting me into this mess when she suggested that I write about something other than ghosts. She said to me, "You love crime history, too. Why don't you write about that?" Thus, my "other" writing began.

A Bloody History of Early Illinois Crime

Illinois was, in many ways, born in blood. From the Indian massacres of the War of 1812 to the feuds and vendettas in the late 1800s, there is a long history of violence and death written in blood during the early days of the state. But almost every part of the country in its early days of scant population was the scene of open crime. Outlaws, fleeing in desperation from the restraints of civilization, where the law was strictly enforced, found the wilderness a region where they could carry on their lawless ways. The settlements in those days were small and widely scattered, with broad spaces of unknown forest and prairie lying in between. The beleaguered upholders of the law, if any such men were even on duty, were unable to be everywhere at once. It was easy in those days to operate in secrecy, and the very life of the frontier bred a class of rough and desperate men, capable of committing almost any crime.

There is likely no part of Illinois that does not have its local traditions of outlawry during its period of early settlement, including the northern reaches of the state. There, tales that were often weird and gruesome were told for years until a time came when popular sentiment became too strong to harbor criminals. Even today, there are locations that are pointed out as murder sites and places where gangs of outlaws once hid. Often, these tales are so filled with lore that it is hard to tell where truth ends and fiction begins. Regardless, they paint a vivid portrait of how Illinois came to be and why it gained such a reputation as a lawless place.

Indian Massacres

The first French explorers came to Illinois in 1763, when an expedition led by Louis Jolliet and Father Jacques Marquette journeyed down the Mississippi River. Jolliet was an explorer and mapmaker, while Marquette was a Jesuit priest who longed to bring his religion to the native people of the wilderness. These two, along with several Indians and nineteen other white men, undertook a treacherous journey that brought them all the way to the mouth of the river. They crossed land on their return journey, paddling northward on the Illinois and Des Plaines Rivers to Lake Michigan, and opened the wilderness of Illinois for the French settlers and adventurers who followed.

Men like LaSalle conquered the region, and from 1698 to 1722, the French expanded throughout the Lower Mississippi Valley. Settlements began to appear at Kaskaskia, Cahokia, St. Genevieve and Fort de Chartres. In 1763, the city of St. Louis was founded, and not long after, settlers, explorers and fur traders flocked to the Illinois country. The region remained under French control for years, until it was given to Spain, returned to France in 1800 and then sold to the United States in 1803.

The years that followed were a period of lawlessness and lack of order for Illinois. The region was initially a part of the state of Virginia and then became the Illinois Territory in 1809. By this time, settlers from the East had started to arrive in the area, and with them came myriad problems and a great threat to the Indian populace. The threat of encroachment, combined with another war with England, led to the first blood being spilled in Illinois.

When the War of 1812 began, the Illinois Territory became an integral part of the fighting. Along the East Coast and the Canadian border, the American forces fought against British invasion. Illinois—at the time, the far western frontier—was left out of this part of the war, but the state was torn apart by terrible massacres and battles with Indian allies of the British, who created more havoc and committed more horrific murders than the British could ever dream of. Shortly after the outbreak of the war, the infamous Fort Dearborn Massacre took place at the site of present-day Chicago.

The site of Fort Dearborn was staked out by Captain John Whistler in April 1803. His orders had been to take six soldiers from the First U.S. Infantry, survey a road from Detroit to the mouth of the river and draw up plans for a fort at this location.

There were sixty-nine officers and men in the contingent that had the task of building Fort Dearborn, named in honor of Secretary of War Henry Dearborn, a man who would go on to be considered one of the most inept leaders in American history. The hill on which Fort Dearborn was built was eight feet above the Chicago River. The water curved around it and, stopped from flowing into a lake by a sandbar, ran south until it found an outlet. To this spot, the soldiers hauled the wood that had been cut along the north bank. The fort was a simple stockade built of logs, which were placed in the ground and then sharpened along the upper end to discourage attackers. The outer stockade was a solid wall with an entrance in the southern section blocked with heavy gates. An underground exit was located on the north side. As time went on, the soldiers built barracks, officers' quarters, a guardhouse and a small powder magazine made from brick. West of the fort, they constructed a two-story log building with split-oak siding to serve as an Indian agency, and between this structure and the fort they placed root cellars. South of the fort, the land was enclosed for a garden. Blockhouses were added at two corners of the fort, and three pieces of light artillery were mounted at the walls. The fort offered substantial protection for the soldiers garrisoned there, but they would later learn that it was not enough.

An illustration showing Fort Dearborn, where a major Indian massacre on the frontier occurred during the War of 1812. *Chicago Historical Society*.

At the start of the War of 1812, tensions in the wilderness began to rise. British troops came to the American frontier, spreading liquor and discontent among the Indian tribes—especially the Potawatomis, the Wyandots and the Winnebagos—near Fort Dearborn. In April, an Indian raid occurred on the Lee Farm, near the bend in the river (where present-day Racine Avenue meets the river), and two men were killed. After that, the fort became a refuge for many of the settlers and a growing cause of unrest for the local Indians. When war was declared that summer and the British captured the American garrison at Mackinac, it was decided that Fort Dearborn could not be held and that it should be evacuated.

General William Hull, the American commander in the Northwest, issued orders to Captain Nathan Heald through Indian agent officers. He was told that the fort was to be abandoned, arms and ammunition destroyed and all goods distributed to friendly Indians. Hull also sent a message to Fort Wayne, which sent Captain William Wells and a contingent of allied Miami Indians toward Fort Dearborn to assist with the evacuation.

There is no dispute about whether General Hull gave the order, nor whether Captain Heald received it, but some have wondered if perhaps Hull's instruction, or his handwriting, was not clear because Heald waited eight days before acting on it. During that time, Heald argued with his officers; with John Kinzie, a settlement trader who opposed the evacuation; and with local Indians, one of whom fired off a rifle in the commanding officer's quarters.

The delay managed to give the hostile Indians time to gather outside the fort. They assembled there in an almost siege-like state, and Heald realized that he was going to have to bargain with them if the occupants of Fort Dearborn were going to safely reach Fort Wayne. On August 13, all of the blankets, trading items and calico cloth were given out, and Heald held several councils with Indian leaders, meetings that his junior officers refused to attend.

Eventually, an agreement was reached in which the Indians would allow safe conduct for the soldiers and settlers to Fort Wayne in Indiana. Part of the agreement was that Heald would leave the arms and ammunition in the fort for the Indians, but his officers, alarmed, questioned the wisdom of handing out guns and ammunition that could easily be turned against them. Heald reluctantly went along with them, and the extra weapons and ammunition were broken apart and dumped into an abandoned well. Only twenty-five rounds of ammunition were saved for each man. As an added bit of insurance, all of the liquor barrels were smashed, and the contents were poured into the river during the night. Some would later claim that Heald's broken promise was what prompted the massacre that followed.

On August 14, Captain William Wells and his Miami allies arrived at the fort. Wells has largely been forgotten today, but at the time he was a frontier legend among soldiers, Native Americans and settlers in the Northwest Territory. Born in 1770, he was living in Kentucky in 1784 when he was kidnapped by a raiding party of Miami Indians. Wells was adopted into the tribe, took a Miami name—Apekonit, or "Carrot Top" for his red hair—and earned a reputation as a fierce warrior. He married into the tribe, and his wife, Wakapanke ("Sweet Breeze") was the daughter of the great Miami leader Little Turtle. The couple eventually had four children and remained together even after Wells left the Miamis and settled at Fort Wayne as the government's Indian agent.

When Wells received word from General Hull about the evacuation of Fort Dearborn, he went straight to Chicago. His niece, Rebekah, was married to the fort's commander, Captain Heald. But even the arrival of the frontiersman and his loyal Miami warriors would not save the lives of those trapped inside Fort Dearborn.

Throughout the night of August 14, wagons were loaded for travel, and the reserve ammunition was distributed. Late in the evening, Captain Heald received a visitor, a Potawatomi named Mucktypoke ("Black Partridge"), who had long been an ally to the Americans. He knew that he could no longer hold back the anger of his fellow tribesmen, and he sadly gave back to Heald the medal of friendship that had been given to him by the U.S. government. He explained to Heald, "I will not wear a token of peace while I am compelled to act as an enemy."

Heald had fair warning that the occupants of Fort Dearborn were in great danger.

Early the next day, a hot and sunny Saturday morning, the procession of soldiers, civilians, women and children left the fort. Leading the way was William Wells, riding a thoroughbred horse. Wells, in honor of his Miami heritage, had painted his face black. He was now a warrior prepared for battle—and for death.

A group of fifteen Miami warriors trailed behind him, followed by the infantry soldiers, a caravan of wagons and mounted men. More of the Miami Indians guarded the rear of the column. The procession included fifty-five soldiers, twelve militiamen, nine women and eighteen children. Some of the women were on horseback, and most of the children rode in two wagons. Two fife players and two drummers played a tune that history has since forgotten, perhaps marching music to inspire the exodus.

The column of soldiers and settlers was escorted by nearly five hundred Potawatomi and Winnebago Indians. In 1812, the main branch of the Chicago River did not follow a straight course into Lake Michigan. Instead, just east of the fort, it curved to the south, struggled around the sand dunes and then emptied into the lake. The shoreline of the lake was then much closer to the present-day line of Michigan Avenue. The column from Fort Dearborn marched southward and into a low range of sand hills (near what is now Roosevelt Road) that separated the beaches of Lake Michigan from the prairie. As it did so, the Potawatomis moved to the right, placing an elevation of sand between themselves and the contingent from the fort. They were now mostly hidden from view.

The procession traveled to an area where Sixteenth Street and Indiana Avenue are now located. There was a sudden milling about of the scouts at the front of the line, and suddenly a shout came back from Captain Wells that the Indians were attacking. Captain Heald ordered his troops to charge, and the soldiers scurried up the dunes with bayonets fixed, breaking the Potawatomi line. The Indians fell back, allowed the soldiers in and then enveloped them. Soldiers fell immediately, and the line collapsed. Eventually, the remaining men retreated to the shoreline, making a defensive stand on a high piece of ground, but the Potawatomis overwhelmed them with sheer numbers.

The soldiers' charge led them away from the wagons, leaving only the twelve-man militia to defend the women and children. Desperate to protect the families, the men fired their rifles until they were out of ammunition and then swung them like clubs before they were all slain. What followed was butchery. A Potawatomi climbed into the wagon with the children and bludgeoned them to death with his tomahawk. The fort's surgeon was cut down by gunfire and then literally chopped into pieces. Rebekah Heald was wounded seven times but was spared when she was captured by a sympathetic Indian chief. The wife of one soldier fought so bravely and savagely that she was hacked into pieces before she fell.

Aware of the slaughter taking place at the wagons, William Wells rushed to the aid of the women and children. Overcome by the massive number of Potawatomis, he never made it. Wells was said to have fought more than one hundred Indians, single-handed and on horseback. He shot and hacked at them until his horse fell beneath him. Indians pounced on him and killed him in the sand. One Potawatomi took Wells's scalp, while another cut out his heart, divided it into small pieces and gave them to other warriors. Honoring the slain hero, and hoping to gain a small amount of his great courage, they ate the heart of William Wells.

Then a Potawatomi attacked Margaret Helm, the wife of the fort's lieutenant. As the two fought, a second Potawatomi joined the fight, seized Mrs. Helm and dragged her into the lake, where he proceeded to drown her—or that was how it appeared. The second warrior was Black Partridge, a close friend of Lieutenant Helm. The pretend drowning was actually a ruse to save her life.

Although it must have seemed much longer, the battle was over in less than fifteen minutes. Captain Heald, who had been wounded twice in the fighting and would walk with a cane for the rest of his life, agreed to parlay with Potawatomi chief Black Bird. After receiving assurances that the survivors would be spared, Heald agreed to surrender. Sixty-seven people had lost their lives in the massacre: William Wells, twenty-five army regulars, all twelve militiamen, twelve children, two women and fifteen Potawatomis.

The surrender that was arranged by Captain Heald did not apply to the wounded, and it is said that the Indians tortured them throughout the night and then left their bodies on the sand next to those who had already fallen.

Many of the other survivors suffered terribly. The Potawatomis divided up the prisoners, and most were eventually ransomed and returned to their families. Others did not fare so well. One man was tomahawked when he could not keep pace with the rest of the group being marched away from the massacre site. A baby who cried too much during the march was tied to a tree and left to starve. Mrs. Isabella Cooper was scalped before being rescued by an Indian woman. She had a small bald spot on her head for the rest of her life. Another man froze to death that winter, while Mrs. John Simmons and her daughter were forced to run a gauntlet, which both survived. In fact, the girl turned out to be the last survivor of the massacre; she died in 1900.

Captain Heald, along with his wife, was also taken prisoner. He and Rebekah were taken to Fort Mackinac and were turned over to the British commander there. The commander sent them to Detroit, where they were exchanged with the American authorities.

After the carnage, the victorious Indians burned Fort Dearborn to the ground, and the bodies of the massacre victims were left where they had fallen, scattered to decay on the sand dunes of Lake Michigan. When replacement troops arrived at the site a year later, they were greeted with not only the burned-out shell of the fort but also the grinning skeletons of their predecessors. In 1816, the bodies were finally given a proper burial, likely around present-day Prairie Avenue and Seventeenth Street, and the fort was rebuilt. Twenty years later, the fort was finally abandoned when the city of Chicago was able to fend for itself.

Those days at the start of the war were dark ones for the Illinois territory, but the years that followed were no brighter. Immediately after the massacre at Fort Dearborn, British officials started down the Mississippi River spreading gifts, liquor and discontent among the Indians. In retaliation, Illinois' territorial governor, Ninian Edwards, gathered a group of 350 frontiersmen at Camp Russell (near present-day Edwardsville) and organized them as mounted riflemen. They were reinforced by three companies of United States Rangers under the command of Colonel Russell. The troops advanced north along the Illinois River, burning Indian settlements and slaughtering any of the inhabitants who fought back. When the men returned to Camp Russell, only one of the soldiers had been wounded.

By the dawn of 1813, Illinois had fortified, and settlers prepared for the worst. Blockhouses and forts had appeared along the frontier, and settlers in remote locations were evacuated to safety. New companies of rangers were formed and posted at positions all over the territory, but this was not enough to stop the marauding Indians. Along the Mississippi, from present-day Alton to Kaskaskia, twenty-two forts were built for defense, but the Indians slipped through and attacked the Lively family, who lived four miles south of Covington. The attackers offered no mercy. Lively was mutilated and murdered, and his wife and daughter were raped, ravaged and killed. One of his sons, a child of seven, was dragged from the house and beheaded. Another of the Lively sons, along with a stranger who had been passing by and having dinner with the family, escaped and summoned help. A company of rangers under Captain Bond pursued the Indians, but they vanished into the wilderness.

A few days after the Lively Massacre, two men were murdered near the present-day town of Carlyle, and then several more attacks followed on the Cache River, on the Wabash and near the present-day town of Albion, in Edwards County. Another military expedition was formed in response and was sent north to the area around Peoria Lake, where a large number of Native Americans had gathered and were using the area as a staging point for attacks across the territory. A group of nine hundred men was sent, under the command of General Howard of the U.S. Army, to rendezvous with troops from Missouri under Colonel McNair. The Missouri men marched one hundred miles on the western side of the Mississippi to Fort Madison, where they swam the river naked and mounted their horses while their clothing and guns were rafted across. The troops, now banded together, continued their northward march.

Near present-day Quincy, they turned east, headed to the mouth of the Spoon River and then followed the Illinois to Peoria, where they found a small stockade commanded by Captain Nicholas. The stockade had been attacked just two days before, but Nicholas and his men had managed to fight off the Indians. The expedition continued on but found only deserted villages as they marched. The raiders had apparently moved on to another location. The entire expedition turned out to be bloodless, but it did manage to temporarily halt the attacks on the Illinois settlers.

Despite the best efforts of the rangers and the frontier defenders, the atrocities and attacks continued. The war was beginning to turn against the British by the early months of 1814, and after their defeat at the Battle of Thames, most of the hostile Indians were driven away from the Canadian border. This was a good sign for overall victory in the war, but it had dire results for Illinois settlers. Indians began to gather along the Upper Mississippi and started attacking small Illinois settlements.

In July, a band of Indians attacked the homes of two families who had settled between the forks of the Wood River, not far from the present-day site of Alton. On July 10, marauders killed two of Abel Moore's children, two of William Moore's children and two children and the wife of Reason Reagan. The Moores and the Reagans were two of the ten families who had started farms in the area about 1810.

The attacks occurred on Sunday, July 10, while Reagan was away at church. He left his wife, Rachel, and two children, Elizabeth and Timothy, at the home of Abel Moore. Late in the day, Rachel left to return to her own home and took all of the children present with her, including the two sons of William Moore and two children of Abel Moore. Another young woman, Hannah Bates, planned to accompany her but turned back because her feet were hurting from a new pair of shoes. Tragically, the rest of the party never reached the Reagan home.

Shortly after nightfall, William Moore realized that his children had never come home, and he began to search for them. He and his wife took different routes in their search. Moore soon stumbled over a body in the darkness but could not identify it. His wife was not so fortunate. She found the bloodied corpses of Rachel Reagan and her son Timothy and returned home in a state of hysteria.

At dawn, a party from a nearby blockhouse took up the search, and the mangled bodies of the missing settlers were discovered within a mile of the protection offered by the fort. The bodies were wrapped in winding sheets, since there was no one available to build coffins, and interred in a common grave.

Captain Samuel Whiteside, along with a company of rangers, pursued the Indians, following them as far as the Sangamon River. They fought near the present-day site of Virden, but only one of the Indians was killed. Tucked into the dead man's belt, they found the blood-soaked scalp of Rachel Reagan. The rest of the killers vanished into the forest.

Throughout 1814, more attacks took place along the frontier, and dozens of additional settlers were killed. In August, the rangers struck back and attacked a war party near the site of the Lively Massacre, which had occurred the previous year. All of the Indians were killed, and only one ranger was lost in the skirmish.

The end of that year brought a close to the war, and afterward, a strong movement began to bring settlers to the region and to move the Native Americans out. The white men were rarely honest when it came to business dealings with the Indians, and large portions of land were purchased for small amounts of money. In many cases, the Indians were just driven out altogether. Although the last treaty relocating the Indians would not be signed until the 1830s, the federal government already controlled most of Illinois by 1818, when it was decided to make the territory into a state.

BANDITS AND HIGHWAYMEN

Although river pirates frequently prowled the waters of Southern Illinois, the greatest danger to travelers and settlers during the days of early Northern Illinois was the threat of robbery and murder on land. Bandits and highwaymen prowled the roadways of the state, especially in the sparsely populated areas. These regions were often scenes of open crime. The persistent myth of the "good old days" in which our ancestors lived finds little support in the annals of Illinois crime during the early and mid-1800s.

There is likely no county in the state without its local traditions of organized outlawry in its early years. Author Milo M. Quaife quoted a western traveler who came to Illinois in 1819:

> *Illinois is the hiding place for villains from every part of the United States and, indeed, from every quarter of the globe. A majority of the settlers have been discharged from penitentiaries and jails or have been the victims of misfortune or imprudence. Many of those will reform, but many, very many, are made fit for robbery and murder.*

This may have been a bit of an overstatement, but it is clear that throughout the early days of Illinois, crimes of violence were alarmingly prevalent. The

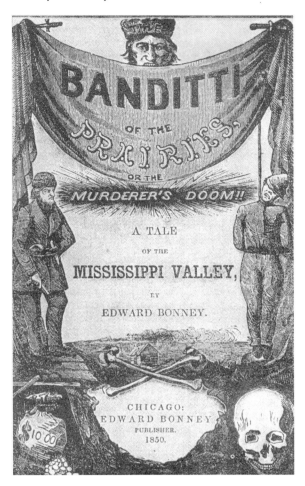

The title page of an 1850 book by Edward Bonney about the notorious cutthroats who roamed Illinois during the middle part of the 1800s.

chief crime among them was robbery, and Illinois during the 1840s and 1850s was infested by organized bands of cutthroats who brought terror to travelers and law-abiding citizens throughout the region. The two things most commonly sought were horses and money. Murder often occurred, although it was unlikely in connection to horse theft. Horses were easily passed on to confederates in some section remote from the crime for disposal to innocent buyers. The victim only knew that he had been robbed and had slight chance of tracing his property, or proving ownership if he did.

The stealing of money involved either robbery from the person or theft of homes. In cases of the latter kind, the method of operation was simple. There was a widespread mistrust of banks in those days, and anyone with extra funds usually hid them somewhere in their home. This circumstance was likely to be known, or at least suspected, by neighbors, who also knew the layout of the house and the members of the potential victim's family. Any neighbor with criminal inclinations (and they were not hard to find) could pass this information on to a professional bandit, who would commit the robbery and depart the area after paying off the helpful neighbor for his part in the crime. If all went well, the crime would be one of simple burglary, but if some member of the household chanced to interrupt it, a murder was likely to follow.

Crime obviously affected everyone in the region at that time, but strangers and travelers were especially in danger. A man might be robbed and killed in the settlement where he lived, but this could hardly be done without it becoming known to his friends and neighbors, who were likely to alert the authorities and bring about whatever justice was available at the time. A traveler from some distant place, however, was almost completely cut off from all who knew him. If his appearance or conversation were such to make people think he was possessed of some means, he made a promising potential victim to the criminals who frequented the taverns and highways. Such a person was liable to vanish without any explanation, and no one would be the wiser.

Murders and disappearances became common, and records of the time make it painfully clear that people had every right to be concerned. One gang of outlaws that operated in Northern Illinois eventually fled the region but left a number of chilling items behind. Among the effects found abandoned in the gang's headquarters were a suspiciously large number of trunks, cases and empty containers that had once belonged to travelers, peddlers and businessmen. This discovery was generally believed to account for the fate of salesmen and other travelers who, at various times, had been known to come into the community and had mysteriously vanished from sight.

Samuel J. Low, who was twice elected sheriff of Cook County in the 1840s, wrote:

> *Organized bands of counterfeiters, horse thieves and desperate men, versed in crime of every character, abounded. For every head of the serpent crushed, another was raised. Every grove to the Wabash might have been said to contain caches of stolen goods and horses, and the cellar of many a tavern the bones of murdered men.*

REGULATORS AND VIGILANCE SOCIETIES

During the 1840s and 1850s, outlaw gangs were so rampant in Illinois that the legal authorities were utterly powerless to convict them. They could do nothing to combat the wide influence that the outlaws had in the places where they lived and where businesses depended on them spending their ill-gotten gains. Pitched battles between the bandits and officers of the law frequently took place. Murders were carried out to keep witnesses from testifying, and courthouses were burned to destroy evidence. Many counties spent months in a literal state of terror. These events continued unchecked until the people themselves formed bands of "regulators," vigilante societies that hanged or drove out the worst offenders.

Regulators and vigilante groups began to appear in every corner of the state, formed for the purpose of ridding the country of undesirable characters. Even law enforcement officials felt these men were largely justified by the circumstances. The entire region had been nearly overrun by counterfeiters, horse thieves, highway robbers and killers; small towns were invaded by robbers in search of plunder; and isolated merchants were held up at gunpoint. In many counties, the outlaws were so numerous and well organized that they openly defied the law. Sheriffs, justices of the peace, judges and constables numbered among the lawbreakers, and numerous friends in high places shielded them from punishment. When arrested, they escaped easily from poorly constructed jails, bribed juries or used lying witnesses to prove themselves innocent. Conviction, by any usual procedure, was practically impossible.

It was under these intolerable conditions that the people finally took the law into their own hands. The governor and most of the judges in the region, realizing the necessity of such action, largely ignored the vigilantes and allowed them freedom to operate. The regulators, as Governor Ford described them, formed and elected officers as a militia would. Their operations were conducted almost entirely at night, and they went about armed to the teeth. When they tracked down criminals, they arrested, tried and punished them on the spot. The usual punishments were whippings and banishment from the region, although there were many instances when offenders were promptly hanged from the nearest tree.

In most districts, this method worked well, but some parts of Northern Illinois were worse than others. Well-organized bands operated for many years north of the Illinois River, engaged in murder, horse stealing, robbery and counterfeiting. While few areas were completely free of criminals, the largest groups of them congregated in Ogle, Winnebago, Lee and DeKalb

An old Illinois courthouse near Peoria in the 1850s. In buildings like this, bandits and outlaws were tried in vain for the crimes they had committed. The frustration of the residents, who wanted to see these men punished for their crimes, eventually led to the formation of vigilante groups.

Counties. In Ogle County, they became so numerous and so powerful that any conviction for crime was rendered impossible.

In the spring term of 1841, seven well-known outlaws were confined in the Ogle County Jail. The judge and lawyers involved in their cases had assembled in Oregon to hold proceedings in the new courthouse that had just been completed there. During the night, a gang of outlaw sympathizers set fire to the new building, hoping, in the ensuing excitement, to rescue the prisoners. The jailbreak failed, but the new courthouse was completely destroyed. The public was outraged, and taking advantage of this sentiment, the court convened; three of the prisoners were tried, convicted and sentenced to the penitentiary. During the trial, one of the outlaws' confederates managed to get onto the jury and refused to agree on a verdict until the other jury members threatened to hang him in the jury room. The four other prisoners obtained changes of venue and were never brought to trial. They managed to break out of jail and escape.

The entire affair so aroused the law-abiding citizens of the area that they resolved to take the law into their own hands. They were determined that insecure jails, changes of venue, hung juries and perjured evidence would no longer protect criminals from justice. All over Ogle and Winnebago Counties, vigilance committees were created, and these companies of regulators set to work hunting down criminals, punishing them and forcing them out of the region.

Among those banished by the Ogle County Lynching Club, as the vigilantes called themselves, were John Driscoll, who lived in the northeastern part of the county, and his sons, William and David, who lived a few miles away. The father and his offspring had spent time in the Ohio Penitentiary and were known thieves. The family was determined not to be driven away and, joining with several others of their ilk, resolved to strike back at the regulators. The first captain of the regulators was John Long, who owned a mill. His mill was burned to the ground, and he resigned his commission. In his place was chosen Captain John Campbell, a rough-and-tumble Scotsman who would not be easily bullied. Campbell led a large contingent of armed men into western Dekalb County and, when questioned about their intentions by law officers, replied that they planned to drive the criminals from the country. The lawmen sent them on their way, making no objections to their plans.

The incident sealed the fate of Captain Campbell, however. When word reached the outlaws, they wanted to make it clear that they would do more than burn the mills of the men who opposed them.

One Sunday evening, near dark, some of the Driscoll Gang went to Captain Campbell's house in White Rock Grove. Pretending to be strangers who needed directions, they called their victim outside and then shot him to death in front of his wife and children. Witnesses believed that two of the gunmen were David and Taylor Driscoll.

Before daybreak, the news of the murder had spread all over the region. Regulators, and men who were sympathetic to their cause, flocked to Campbell's house and made plans to avenge the death of their fallen leader. David and Taylor Driscoll had vanished, but John Driscoll was taken, and his house was burned to the ground. Another group of regulators captured William Driscoll and his younger brother, Pierce. The two of them were taken to Captain Campbell's home, and Campbell's widow was asked to identify the men. She stated that they were not the killers, but her words fell on deaf ears. Such emotion had risen against the Driscolls that they were taken prisoner along with the other members of the family.

The next day, the Driscolls were taken by wagon—with ropes around their necks—to a spot where a trial could be held. A barrel of whiskey was procured from a local distillery, and the regulators freely imbibed while waiting for a lawyer named Leland to arrive. He would act as the judge in the case. John Driscoll was given a short trial and sentenced to death. William was then led into the ring, and Leland invited accusations to be leveled against him. There was little that could be said, especially given that Campbell's widow would not speak against him. A number of citizens from Sycamore, convinced of his innocence, spoke on his behalf but were booed and hissed at until they fell silent. Eventually, William's fate was sealed when a general cry from the crowd called for his death.

Only the boy, Pierce, was spared. His youth, combined with no evidence against him at all, moved the crowd to mercy, and he was released.

The two condemned men were given an hour to prepare for their deaths, and a Methodist minister, who was present as the leader of the regulators in Oregon, drank a dipper of whiskey and then knelt down with them for a lengthy prayer. William Driscoll prayed along with the minister, but his father looked on in disgust. At the appointed time, they were forced to kneel in front of the entire company. Every man present fired his rifle at them so that none could be a legal witness of the deed. The two Driscolls were cut down by the hail of bullets and instantly killed. Their bodies were unceremoniously thrown into a brush heap, and the regulators returned to their homes.

The regulators provided a crude, yet serviceable remedy for a disease that was plaguing Northern Illinois. An innocent man, in all probability, had gone to his death alongside his guilty father, yet the executions of two members of the Driscoll family broke up the criminal gang and returned a semblance of peace to a beleaguered region.

The Murder of Colonel Davenport

One of the most sensational crimes of the 1840s in Northern Illinois was the July 4, 1845 murder of Colonel George Davenport. Davenport was a British immigrant who came to America in 1804. He served in the military for a time and then came west, running supplies on the Mississippi River between St. Louis and Fort Armstrong, which was being built on an island between Illinois and Iowa. He eventually brought his wife, Margaret, with him to Fort Armstrong, and there they raised a family as Davenport established trading posts on the river and created strong ties with the Winnebago Indians, who referred to him as Saganosh, meaning "Englishman." Relations between the Native Americans and most of the settlers were not so friendly, however, and problems started with Black Hawk, a chief of the Sac Nation, who wanted the white men removed from his land. Davenport, fearing trouble for both sides, traveled to Washington to speak to President Andrew Jackson on behalf of the Indians.

Despite this attempt to broker peace, violence broke out in the early 1830s, and troops were sent in to protect the settlers. Davenport was appointed quartermaster officer with the rank of colonel in the Illinois militia, and Fort Armstrong became the headquarters for General Winfield Scott's army during the Black Hawk War. After several bloody skirmishes, the war ended in the summer of 1832 with the capture of Chief Black Hawk and the forced sale of Native American lands to the government.

After the war, the nearby Illinois settlement of Farnhamsburg grew rapidly, and there was a proposal to establish a larger town and name it Davenport in the colonel's honor. However, during the Black Hawk War, Davenport had verbally opposed the tactics of Colonel Stroud, tactics that he felt led to greater violence and bloodshed. After the war, Stroud became a member of the Illinois legislature and refused to allow the town to be named Davenport. Stroud saw to it that it was named Stephenson instead, after Colonel James Stephenson. Six years later, its name was changed again to Rock Island.

In 1835, a company was formed to start a new town in Iowa, directly across the river from Stephenson. Its representatives met at Colonel Davenport's island mansion and surveyed and laid out the town, which they called Davenport. Fort Armstrong was evacuated in 1836, having outlived its usefulness, and control of the site was transferred to Colonel Davenport, who remained in charge until 1840. At that time, it became a national arms depot, the Rock Island Arsenal, which was used for the deposit and repair of munitions.

Colonel Davenport was murdered on July 4, 1845. The rest of his family had gone to the big Independence Day celebration in the city of Rock Island, but Davenport stayed home. A few minutes after 1:00 p.m., he went out for a pitcher of water, and when he returned, he heard a noise in the next room. Davenport went to investigate and was immediately confronted by several men who had broken into the house. They had been lured to the house by the rumor of more than $200,000 that Davenport supposedly kept in his safe. One of the men fired a pistol at him, and Davenport was wounded in the thigh. Having no guns at hand, he rushed back into his office and tried to get to his cane. He seized it and turned to strike at the closest assailant but was thrown to the floor. His hands were tied, and he was blindfolded as the thieves rummaged through his desk, looking for the iron keys to the safe. The safe was located upstairs, and when the men were unable to unlock it, they dragged Davenport up the staircase by his heels and forced him to open it for them. The contents of the safe turned out not to be the vast fortune they expected. Instead, they found only about $500 in Missouri bills inside.

Davenport was then dragged back into his office and beaten and tortured until he revealed the location of more cash. He choked out the directions to a drawer in his desk, but the thieves opened the wrong one and found only a small amount of money. They never realized their mistake. Convinced there was no more money to be found, the bandits began arguing about what to do with the colonel. Two of the men wanted to kill him and burn down the house, but a third man—likely the one who shot him, although Davenport could not be sure since he was blindfolded—urged the others to forget about him. Finally, they left him behind in a pool of blood as they ransacked the rest of the house.

The Murder of Colonel Davenport

The home of Colonel Davenport on Rock Island, where he was robbed and murdered.

A few friends stopped at the house just a short time after the robbers had departed and discovered Davenport in his office, bleeding badly. A doctor was summoned, but the gunshot wound, combined with the beating that he took, was too much for him to bear. Davenport lingered until about 9:00 p.m. that night, breathing and speaking with great difficulty before he finally expired. He was buried on the land near his mansion on July 5, after a ceremony conducted by Fox Indians, with whom he was friendly. A second funeral service, performed by Dr. Goldsmith from the Episcopal Church, was held later in the day for everyone to attend.

The public was outraged by the crime, and the authorities relentlessly pursued the killers. John Baxter, John Long, Aaron Long, Granville Young and William Fox were all charged with the murder. Robert Burch, William Redden and Grant Redden were all charged as accessories after the fact.

William Fox was captured first, on September 8, in Wayne County, Indiana. He was brought in irons to Rock Island but somehow managed to escape and was never found. Robert Burch and John Long were arrested on September 19 in Sandusky, Ohio, and were also returned to Rock Island. Burch was arrested carrying a watch and gold chain that belonged to Colonel Davenport and was also the same man accused of robbing another Rock Island man named Mulford sometime before the Davenport murder.

The Reddens were arrested after two guns belonging to Davenport were found in their possession by one of the colonel's sons. The Reddens lived near Fort Madison, at the mouth of Devil's Creek, and a number of men went there to arrest them. They were met by great resistance, but after a pitched battle, the Reddens, along with Granville Young, were captured. Young was believed to have taken part in the robbery, and the Reddens were accused of harboring the killers after the murder had taken place. Apparently, their home was used as a rendezvous point for many outlaws who operated in the area. Later, Grant Redden was cleared of all charges, but William Redden ended up spending one year in the penitentiary.

John Baxter and Aaron Long were also arrested a short time later. Baxter had been captured at the home of his brother-in-law, Berry Haney, of Madison, Wisconsin. He had been a resident of the Rock Island area for many years and always had a good reputation, up until the time of the murder. Baxter, whom the newspapers said appeared to be "grief-stricken," made a full confession about his role in the murder. He gave many people the impression that he was a good man who got caught up in unfortunate circumstances.

Long, on the other hand, was not a sympathetic character. He had been blatantly associated with many of Illinois' outlaw gangs. At the time of his arrest, he and his father, who was also supposed to be a notorious gang member, were residing in a boardinghouse about six miles from Galena.

Robert Burch turned state's evidence in the case and ended up with reduced charges of being an accessory. There was no question that he was involved in the robbery after he disclosed to the police where some of the loot had been hidden. He was taken to the spot in chains and was returned to the jail after the valuables had been recovered. Burch testified against the others involved in the crime, and they were all indicted by a grand jury soon after. Burch was later convicted and sentenced to a life term in prison, but he escaped and was killed three months later.

John Baxter, John Long, Aaron Long, Granville Young and William Fox were all found guilty after just two hours of deliberation by a jury. All of the men were sentenced to hang on October 30. The prisoners were taken to the gallows, and then, with their hands tied and hoods placed over their heads, the rope was cut, sending them to their deaths. Strangely, though, the rope around Aaron Long's neck snapped, and he fell heavily to the ground beneath the scaffold. Sympathy was immediately created in his favor as he was led back to the scaffold, pleading that his life be spared. Some members of the assembled crowd cried out in his defense, but most simply watched in silence as another rope was strung and he was forced to stand on a wooden plank that was placed over the gallows opening. Without fanfare, the board was kicked away, and this time, the rope stretched taut and claimed his life. A hush fell over the few vocal members of the crowd as his feet kicked a few times and then went still.

It was, many of the witnesses believed, a fitting end to the outlaws who killed one of the great leaders of early Northern Illinois.

Stealing the President

The Attempt to Kidnap Abraham Lincoln's Bones

After President Abraham Lincoln was assassinated in April 1865, his body traveled west from Washington, spending several weeks visiting towns and cities along a circuitous route. His funeral service in Springfield did not take place until May 4, and it followed a parade route from the former Lincoln home to Oak Ridge Cemetery, on the far edge of the city. But it would be many years before Lincoln was allowed to rest in peace. His tomb has long been a place of mystery, intrigue and strange speculation.

The mystery began in 1876 with an attempted theft that would cause Lincoln's body to be hidden in one place after another for the next two decades. Lincoln was finally laid to rest in 1901, but the disturbance that shattered his peace got its start many years before with the arrest of a counterfeiter named Benjamin Boyd.

Oak Ridge Cemetery was started in Springfield about 1860 and mostly consisted of woods and unbroken forest. In fact, it wasn't until after Lincoln was buried there that much was done in the way of improvement, adding roads, iron gates and a caretaker's residence. Lincoln himself had chosen the rural graveyard as his final resting place, a fact that city leaders initially balked at. However, pressure from his high-strung widow eventually forced them to go along with his wishes.

Lincoln was placed in a temporary receiving vault in the cemetery with his sons, Willie, who had died during the presidency, and Eddie, who had died many years before. Willie's body had accompanied his father's from Washington, while Eddie's had been exhumed and brought over from another cemetery. A short time later, a temporary vault was built for Lincoln,

President Abraham Lincoln.
National Archives.

Crowds filled Oak Ridge
Cemetery on the day that
Lincoln was interred in a
temporary receiving vault.
His body would remain there
until his permanent monument
could be built. *Illinois State
Historical Library.*

and on December 21, he was placed inside. Six of Lincoln's friends wanted to be sure the body was safe, so a plumber's assistant named Leon P. Hopkins made an opening in the lead box for them to peer inside. All was well, and Lincoln and his sons were allowed a temporary rest. Hopkins stated in a newspaper story of the time, "I was the last man to look upon the face of Abraham Lincoln." Of course, he had no idea at the time just how many others would look upon the president's face in the years to come.

Construction on a permanent tomb for Lincoln lasted more than five years, and on September 19, 1871, the caskets of Lincoln and his sons were removed from the hillside crypt and taken to the catacomb of the new tomb. The plumber, Leon P. Hopkins, opened the coffin once more, and the same six friends peered again at the president's face. There were several crypts waiting for Lincoln and his sons, although one of them had already been filled. Tad Lincoln had died in Chicago a short time before, and his body had already been placed in the nearly finished monument.

Lincoln's tomb at Oak Ridge Cemetery, about 1877. *Illinois State Historical Library.*

During the move, it was noticed that Lincoln's mahogany coffin was beginning to deteriorate, so his friends brought in a new iron coffin, into which the inner coffin of lead, containing Lincoln's body, was transferred. The dead president was laid to rest again, for another three years, while the workmen toiled away outside.

On October 9, 1874, Lincoln was moved again. This time, his body was placed inside a marble sarcophagus, which had been placed in the center of the semicircular catacomb. A few days later, the monument was finally dedicated. The citizens of Springfield seemed content with the final resting place of their beloved Abraham Lincoln. But then a threat arose from a direction that no one could have ever predicted—a plot to steal the body and hold it for ransom! This event became one of the strangest stories in the annals of Illinois crime.

The events began with the arrest of Benjamin Boyd, a petty criminal who had, by 1875, established himself as one of the most skilled engravers of counterfeit currency plates in the country. Boyd had been doggedly pursued by Captain Patrick D. Tyrell of the Chicago office of the U.S. Secret Service for eight months before he was finally captured in Fulton, Illinois, on October 20. Following his trial, Boyd was sentenced to a term of ten years at the Joliet Penitentiary.

Shortly after Boyd's arrest, the strange events concerning the body of Abraham Lincoln began in Lincoln, Illinois. The city was a staging point for a successful gang of counterfeiters run by James "Big Jim" Kneally. The place was an ideal refuge for Kneally's "shovers," pleasant-looking fellows who traveled around the country and passed, or shoved, bogus money to merchants. It has been said that, about this time, at least half of the currency being used in Logan County was counterfeit. Following Boyd's arrest, in the spring of 1876, business took a downturn for the Kneally Gang. With the gang's master engraver in prison, its supply of money was dwindling fast. Things were looking desperate when Kneally seized on a gruesome plan. He would have his men kidnap a famous person and, for a ransom, negotiate for the release of Benjamin Boyd from Joliet prison. Kneally found the perfect candidate as his kidnapping victim: Abraham Lincoln, or at least his famous corpse.

Kneally placed Thomas J. Sharp in charge of assembling the gang and leading the operation. Sharp was the editor of the local *Sharp's Daily Statesman* newspaper and a valued member of the counterfeiting gang. Meanwhile, Kneally returned to St. Louis, where he owned a legitimate livery business, so that he could be far away from suspicion, and have an airtight alibi, as events unfolded. In June, the plan was hammered together at Robert Splain's saloon in Lincoln. Five of the gang members were sent to Springfield to open a saloon that could be used as a base of operations.

This new place was soon established as a tavern and dance hall on Jefferson Street, the site of Springfield's infamous Levee District, a lawless section of town where all manner of vice flourished. Splain served as the bartender while the rest of the gang loitered there as customers. They made frequent visits to the Lincoln Tomb at Oak Ridge, where they found the custodian, John C. Power, more than happy to answer questions about the building. On one occasion, he innocently let slip that there was no guard at the tomb during the night. This clinched the last details of the plan, which involved stealing the body and spiriting it away out of town. It would be buried about two miles north of the city, under a Sangamon River bridge, and then the men would scatter and wait for Kneally to negotiate the ransom. They chose the night of July 3, 1876, to carry out their plan.

The Springfield saloon was up and running by the middle of June, leaving the men with several weeks to do nothing but sit around the tavern, drink and wait. One night, one of the men got very drunk and spilled the details of the plan to a prostitute, who worked at a nearby "parlor house." He told her to look for a little extra excitement in the city on Independence Day. He and his companions planned to steal Lincoln's body while the rest of the city was celebrating the holiday. The story was too good to keep, and the woman passed it along to several other people, including the city's chief of police, Abner Wilkinson, although no record exists of how these two knew each other. The story spread rapidly, and Kneally's men disappeared.

Kneally didn't give up on the plan, however. He simply went looking for more competent help. He moved his base of operations to a tavern called the Hub at 294 West Madison Street in Chicago. Kneally's man there was named Terence Mullen, and he operated a secret headquarters for the gang in the

John C. Power, custodian of the Lincoln Tomb. *Illinois State Historical Library.*

Terence Mullen, one of Kneally's men and the owner of the tavern, the Hub, in Chicago. *Illinois State Historical Library.*

John "Jack" Hughes, another of Kneally's men and a Lincoln tomb robber. *Illinois State Historical Library.*

back room of the tavern. One of Kneally's operatives, Jack Hughes, came into the Hub in August and learned that a big job was in the works. Kneally wanted to steal Lincoln's corpse as soon as possible. Hughes and Mullen had no desire to do this by themselves, so they brought another man into the mix. His name was Jim Morrissey, and he had a reputation for being one of the most skilled grave robbers in Chicago. They decided he would be perfect for the job. Unknown to the gang, Morrissey was actually a Secret Service operative named Lewis Swegles. He had a minor criminal background and had served time for horse stealing. After his release, he went to work as an undercover agent for Captain Patrick Tyrell. When he heard what was happening with the counterfeit gang, he posed as a grave robber.

In 1876, grave robbery was still a national horror and would remain that way for some years to come. Illinois, like most other states, had no laws against the stealing of bodies. It did, however, have a statute that prevented selling the bodies that were taken. Needless to say, this put medical schools in dire need. They often had to depend on "ghouls," or grave robbers, to provide fresh corpses for their anatomy classes. These ghouls had become the terror of communities, and friends and relatives of bereaved families sometimes patrolled graveyards for several nights after a funeral, with shotguns in hand.

Swegles, pretending to be Jim Morrissey, came into the Hub and discussed the methods of grave robbery with the other two men. The three of them quickly devised a plan. They would approach the Lincoln monument under the cover of night and pry open the marble sarcophagus. They would then place the casket in a wagon and drive northward to the Indiana sand dunes. This area was still remote enough to provide a suitable hiding place for however long was needed. Swegles, being the most experienced of the group, agreed to everything about the plan, except for the number of men needed. He believed the actual theft would be harder than they thought and wanted to bring in a famous criminal friend of his to help them. The man's name was Billy Brown, and he could handle the wagon while the others pillaged the tomb. The other two men readily agreed.

On November 5, Mullens and Hughes met with Swegles in his Chicago home for a final conference. They agreed that the perfect night for the robbery would be the night of the upcoming presidential election. The city would be packed with people, and they would be in downtown Springfield very late, waiting near the telegraph and political offices for news. Oak Ridge Cemetery, over two miles away and out in the woods, would be deserted, and the men could work for hours and not be disturbed. It would also be a perfect night to carry the body away, as the roads would be crowded with wagons and people returning home from election celebrations. One more wagon would not be noticed.

The men agreed and decided to leave for Springfield on the next evening's train. Swegles promised to have Billy Brown meet them at the train but felt it was best if he didn't sit with them. He thought that four men might attract too much attention. Hughes and Mullen conceded that this was a good idea but wanted to at least get a look at Brown. Swegles instructed them to stay in their seats, and he would have Brown walk past them to the rear car. As the train was pulling away from the station, a man passed by the two of them and casually nodded his head at them. This was the mysterious fourth man. Brown, after examination, disappeared into the back coach. Hughes and Mullen agreed that he looked fit for the job.

While they were discussing his merits, Billy Brown was hanging onto the back steps of the train and waiting for it to slow down at a crossing on the outskirts of Chicago. At that point, he slipped off the train and headed back into the city. Billy Brown was actually Agent Nealy of the United States Secret Service.

Patrick Tyrell, chief of the Chicago office of the U.S. Secret Service. *Illinois State Historical Library*.

As Nealy was slipping off the train, more agents were taking his place. At the same time the conspirators were steaming toward Springfield, Tyrell and half a dozen operatives were riding in a coach just one car ahead of them. They were also joined on the train by a contingent of Pinkerton detectives, who had been hired by Robert Lincoln after he got word of the plot to steal his father's body. The detectives were led by Elmer Washburne, one of Robert Lincoln's law partners.

A plan was formed between Washburne and Tyrell. Swegles would accompany the grave robbers to Springfield and, while assisting in the robbery, would signal the detectives, who would be hiding in another part of the monument. They would then capture Mullen and Hughes in the act.

When they arrived in Springfield, Tyrell contacted John Todd Stuart, Robert's cousin and the head of the new Lincoln National Monument Association, which cared for the tomb. He advised Stuart of the plan, and together they contacted the custodian of the site. The detectives would hide in the museum side of the monument with the custodian. This area was called Memorial Hall, and it was located on the opposite side of the structure from the catacomb. They would wait there for the signal from Swegles, and then they would rush forward and capture the robbers.

The first Pinkerton agent arrived just after nightfall. He carried with him a note for John Power, the custodian, instructing him to put out the lights and wait for the others to arrive. The two men crouched in the darkness until the other men came inside. Tyrell and his men explored the place with their flashlights. Behind Memorial Hall was a damp, dark labyrinth that wound through the foundations of the monument to a rear wall of the catacomb, where Lincoln was entombed. Against this wall, in the blackness, Tyrell stationed a detective to wait and listen for sounds of the grave robbers. Tyrell then returned to the museum room to wait with the others. Their wait was over as darkness fell outside.

A lantern flashed outside the door, and sounds could be heard as the grave robbers worked at the lock. Almost immediately, Mullen broke the saw blade that he was using on the lock, so they settled in while he resorted to the long and tedious task of filing the lock away. After some time, Mullen finally removed the lock and opened the door to the burial chamber. Before them, in the dim light, they saw the marble sarcophagus of President Lincoln. Now, all they had to do was to remove the lid and carry away the coffin, which turned out to be a much harder task than they had anticipated. The stone was too heavy to move, so using an axe they broke open the top, moved the lid aside and looked into it. Swegles was given the lantern and was stationed nearby to illuminate the work area. Left with no other option, he complied, although he was supposed to light a match at the door to alert the Secret Service agents that it was time to act. Meanwhile, Mullen and Hughes lifted out the heavy casket. Once this was completed, Mullen told Swegles to go and have the wagon moved around. He had assured Mullen and Hughes that Billy Brown had it waiting in a ravine below the hill.

Swegles raced around to Memorial Hall, gave the signal to the detectives and then ran outside. Tyrell whispered to his men, and with drawn revolvers, they rushed out and around the monument to the catacomb. When they arrived, they found the lid to the sarcophagus moved aside and Lincoln's casket on the floor—but the grave robbers were gone!

The detectives scattered outside to search the place. Tyrell ran outside and around the base of the monument, where he saw two men near one of the statues. He whipped up his pistol and fired at them. A shot answered, and they fought it out in a hail of gunfire, dodging around the monument. Suddenly, one of the men at whom he was shooting called out Tyrell's name—he was firing at his own agents!

Mullen and Hughes had casually walked away from the tomb to await the return of Swegles, Brown and the wagon. They never suspected that the whole thing had been a trap. They had only wanted to get some air and had moved into the shadows, where they wouldn't be seen if someone wandered by. After a few minutes, they saw movement at the door to the tomb and started back, thinking that Swegles had returned. They heard the pistol shots and saw a number of men around the monument. They took off running past the ravine and vanished into the night. Assuming that Swegles had been captured, they fled back to Chicago, only to be elated when they found him waiting for them at the Hub tavern. He had returned with the horses, he told them, but found the gang gone. He had come back to Chicago, not knowing what else to do, to await word of what had happened. Thrilled with their good fortune, the would-be grave robbers spent the night in drunken celebration.

The story of the attempted grave robbery appeared in the newspaper following the presidential election, but it was greeted with stunned disbelief. In fact, only one paper, the *Chicago Tribune*, would even print the story because every other newspaper in the state was sure that it was not true. To the general public, the story had to be false, and most believed that it had been hoaxed for some bizarre political agenda. Most people would not believe that the Secret Service and Pinkerton agents would be stupid enough to have gathered all in one room where they could see and hear nothing and then wait for the criminals to act. The Democrats in Congress charged that the Republicans had concocted the whole thing so that it would look like the Democrats had violated the grave of a Republican hero and, in this way, would sway the results of the election. To put it bluntly, no one believed that Lincoln's grave had been, or ever could be, robbed.

The doubters became believers on November 18, when Mullen and Hughes were captured. The newspapers printed the story the following day, and America realized that the story that had appeared a short time before had actually been true. Disbelief turned into horror. Letters poured into the papers, laying the guilt at the feet of everyone—from the Democrats to southern sympathizers to the mysterious John Wilkes Booth Fund.

The people of Illinois were especially outraged, and punishment for the two men would have been severe—if the law had allowed it. After their arrest, the conspirators were placed under heavy guard in the Springfield jail, and on November 20, a special grand jury was convened in Springfield and returned a bill against Mullen and Hughes for attempted larceny and conspiring to commit an unlawful act. There was nothing else they could be charged with. Grave robbery was not a crime in Illinois, and the prosecution, bolstered by Chicago lawyers dispatched by Robert Lincoln, could find no grounds to charge them with anything other than the minor crimes of larceny and conspiracy. Ironically, the charge was not even for conspiring to steal President Lincoln's body. It was actually for planning to steal his coffin, which was the property of the Lincoln National Monument Association.

The public was aghast at the idea that these men would get off so lightly, even though the grand jury had returned a quick indictment. Continuances and changes of venue dragged the case along to May 1877, when it finally came to trial. The jury was asked by the prosecution to sentence the men to the maximum term allowed: five years in prison. On the first ballot, two jurors wanted the maximum; two of them wanted a two-year sentence; four others asked for varying sentences; and four others voted for acquittal. After a few more ballots, Mullen and Hughes were incarcerated for a one-year stay in Joliet.

And Abraham Lincoln was once more left to rest peacefully in his grave, at least for a while.

It was not long before the story of the Lincoln grave robbery became a hotly denied rumor or, at best, a fading legend. The custodians of the site simply decided that it was something they did not wish to talk about. Of course, as the story was denied, the people who had some recollection of the tale created their own truth in myths and conspiracies. The problem in this case, however, was that many of these "conspiracies" happened to be grounded in the truth.

Hundreds of people came to see the Lincoln burial site, and many of them were not afraid to ask about the stories that were being spread about the tomb. From 1876 to 1878, custodian John C. Power gave rather evasive answers to anyone who prodded him for details about the grave robbery. He was terrified of one question in particular, and it seemed to be the one most often asked: was he sure that Lincoln's body had been returned safely to the sarcophagus after the grave robbers took it out?

Power was terrified of that question for one reason: at that time, Lincoln's grave was completely empty.

On the morning of November 1876, when John T. Stuart of the Lincoln National Monument Association learned what had occurred in the tomb with the would-be robbers, he rushed out to the site. He was not able to rest after the incident, fearing that the grave robbers, who had not been caught at that time, would return and finish their ghoulish handiwork. So he made a decision. He contacted the custodian and told him that they must take the body from the crypt and hide it elsewhere in the building. Together, they decided that the best place to store it would be in the cavern of passages that lay between Memorial Hall and the catacomb.

That afternoon, Adam Johnson, a Springfield marble worker, took some of his men and lifted Lincoln's casket from the sarcophagus. They covered it over with a blanket and then cemented the lid back into place. Later that night, Johnson, Power and three members of the Memorial Association stole out to the monument and carried the five-hundred-pound coffin around the base of the obelisk, through Memorial Hall and into the dark labyrinth. They placed the coffin near some boards that had been left behind in the construction. The following day, Johnson built a new outer coffin while Power set to work digging a grave below the dirt floor. It was slow work because it had to be done between visitors to the site, and he also had a problem with water seeping into the hole. Finally, he gave up and simply covered the coffin with the leftover boards and wood.

For the next two years, Lincoln lay beneath a pile of debris in the labyrinth, while visitors from all over the world wept and mourned over the sarcophagus at the other end of the monument. More and more of these visitors asked questions about the theft, questions full of suspicion, as if they knew something they really had no way of knowing.

In the summer and fall of 1877, the legend took another turn. Workmen arrived at the monument to erect the naval and infantry groups of statuary on the corners of the upper deck. Their work would take them into the labyrinth, where Power feared they would discover the coffin. The scandal would be incredible, so Power made a quick decision. He called the workmen together and, swearing them to secrecy, showed them the coffin. They promised to keep the secret, but within days everyone in Springfield seemed to know that Lincoln's body was not where it was supposed to be. Soon, the story was spreading all over the country.

Power was now in a panic. The body had to be more securely hidden, and in order to do that he needed more help. Power contacted two of his friends, Major Gustavas Dana and General Jasper Reece, and explained the situation. These men brought three others—Edward Johnson, Joseph Lindley and James McNeill—to meet with Power.

On the night of November 18, the six men began digging a grave for Lincoln at the far end of the labyrinth. Cramped and cold, and stifled by stale air, they gave up around midnight with the coffin just barely covered and traces of their activity very evident. Power promised to finish the work the next day. These six men, sobered by the responsibility that faced them, decided to form a brotherhood to guard the secret of the tomb. They brought in three younger men—Noble Wiggins, Horace Chapin and Clinton Conkling—to help in the task. They called themselves the Lincoln Guard of Honor and had badges made for their lapels.

After the funeral of Mary Lincoln, John T. Stuart told the Guard of Honor that Robert Lincoln wanted to have his mother's body hidden away with his father's. So, late on the night of July 21, the men slipped into the monument and moved Mary's double-leaded casket, burying it in the labyrinth next to Lincoln's.

Visitors to the tomb increased as the years went by, all of them paying their respects to the two empty crypts. Years later, Power would complain that questions about Lincoln's empty grave were posed to him nearly every day. Finally, in 1886, the Lincoln National Monument Association decided it was time to provide a new tomb for Lincoln in the catacomb. A new and stronger crypt of brick and mortar was designed and made ready.

The press was kept outside as the Guard of Honor, and others who shared the secret of the tomb, brought the Lincoln caskets out of the labyrinth. Eighteen persons who had known Lincoln in life filed past the casket, looking into a square hole that had been cut into the lead coffin. Strangely, Lincoln had changed very little. His face was darker after twenty-two years, but they were still the same sad features these people had always known. The last man to identify the corpse was Leon P. Hopkins, the same man who had closed the casket years before. He soldered the square back over the hole, thinking once again that he would be the last person to ever look upon the face of Abraham Lincoln.

The Guard of Honor lifted Lincoln's casket and placed it next to Mary's smaller one. The two of them were taken into the catacomb and lowered into the new brick and mortar vault. Here, they would sleep for all time.

"All time" lasted for about thirteen more years. In 1899, Illinois legislators decided that the monument was to be torn down and a new one built from the foundation. It seemed that the present structure was settling unevenly, cracking around the "eternal" vault of the president.

There was, once again, the question of what to do with the bodies of the Lincoln family. The Guard of Honor came up with a clever plan. During the fifteen months needed for construction, the Lincolns would be secretly buried in a multiple grave a few feet away from the foundations of the tomb. As the old structure was torn down, tons of stone and dirt would be heaped onto the grave site, both to disguise and protect it. When the new monument was finished, the grave would be uncovered again.

When the new building was completed, the bodies were exhumed once more. In the top section of the grave were the coffins belonging to the Lincoln sons and to a grandson, also named Abraham. The former president and Mary were buried on the bottom level and so safely hidden that one side of the temporary vault had to be battered away to reach them.

Lincoln's coffin was the last to be moved, and it was close to sunset when a steam engine finally hoisted it up out of the ground. The protective outer box was removed, and six construction workers lifted the coffin onto their shoulders and took it into the catacomb. The other members of the family had been placed in their crypts, and Lincoln's casket was placed into a white marble sarcophagus.

The group dispersed after switching on the new electric burglar alarm. This device connected the monument to the caretaker's house, which was a few hundred feet away. As up-to-date as this device was, it still did not satisfy the fears of Robert Lincoln, who was sure that his father's body would be snatched again if care were not taken. He stayed in constant contact with the Guard of Honor, which was still working to ensure the safety of the Lincoln remains, and made a trip to Springfield every month or so after the new monument was completed. Something just wasn't right. Even though the alarm worked perfectly, he could not give up the idea that the robbery might be repeated.

He journeyed to Springfield and brought with him his own set of security plans. He met with officials and gave them explicit directions on what he

Robert Lincoln (seated to the right of E.L. Stanton in 1876) was fiercely protective of the body of his father after the attempted theft of his remains. *Illinois State Historical Library*.

wanted done. The construction company was to break a hole in the tile floor of the monument and place his father's casket at a depth of ten feet. The coffin would then be encased in a cage of steel bars, and the hole would be filled with concrete, making the president's final resting place into a solid block of stone.

On September 26, 1901, a group assembled to make the final arrangements for Lincoln's last burial. A discussion quickly turned into a heated debate. The question that concerned them was whether Lincoln's coffin should be opened and the body viewed one last time. Most felt this would be a wise precaution, especially in light of the continuing stories about Lincoln not being in the tomb. The men of the Guard of Honor were all for laying the tales to rest at last, but Robert was decidedly against opening the casket again, feeling that there was no need to further invade his father's privacy. In the end, practicality won out, and Leon P. Hopkins was sent for to chisel out an opening in the lead coffin. The casket was placed on two sawhorses in the still-unfinished Memorial Hall. The room was described as hot and poorly lighted, as newspapers had been pasted over the windows to keep out the stares of the curious.

A piece of the coffin was cut out and lifted away. According to diaries, a "strong and reeking odor" filled the room, but the group pressed close to the opening anyway. The face of the president was covered with a fine powder made from white chalk. It had been applied in 1865 before the last burial service. It seemed that Lincoln's face had turned inexplicably black in Pennsylvania and, after that, a constant covering of chalk was kept on his face. Lincoln's features were said to be completely recognizable. The casket's headrest had fallen away, and his head was thrown back slightly, revealing his still perfectly trimmed beard. His small black tie and dark hair were still as they had been in life, although his eyebrows had vanished. The broadcloth suit that he had worn to his second inauguration was covered with small patches of yellow mold, and the American flag that was clutched in his lifeless hands was now in tatters.

There was no question, according to those present, that this was Abraham Lincoln and that he was placed in the underground vault. The casket was sealed back up again by Leon Hopkins, making his claim of years earlier true. Hopkins was the last person to look upon the face of Lincoln.

The casket was then lowered down into the cage of steel, and two tons of cement were poured over it, forever encasing the president's body in stone.

This should have been the end of the story, but as with all lingering mysteries, a few questions still remain. The strangest are perhaps these: Does the body of Abraham Lincoln really lie beneath the concrete in the catacomb? Or was the last visit from Robert Lincoln part of some elaborate ruse to throw off any further attempts to steal the president's body? And did Robert, as some rumors have suggested, arrange with the Guard of Honor to have his father's body hidden in a different location entirely?

Most historians would agree that Lincoln's body is safely encased in the concrete of the crypt, but rumors persist. Some might ask whose word we have to support the fact that Lincoln's body is where it is said to be. We only have the statement of Lincoln's son, Robert, his friends and, of course, the Guard of Honor. But weren't these the same individuals who allowed visitors to the monument to grieve before an empty sarcophagus, while the president's body was actually hidden in the labyrinth, beneath a few inches of dirt?

It is a mystery—although perhaps an unlikely one—that refuses to go away.

The Tragic Case of Charles "Pacer" Smith

The idea of professional athletes getting mixed up with the law is nothing new. In fact, incidents of violent crimes go back almost to the beginning of professional sports. During the latter part of the nineteenth century, at least three major-league baseball players committed murder. Edgar McNabb and Marty Bergen killed themselves before they could be brought to trial, and Charlie Sweeney spent several years in San Quentin Prison. On Friday, November 29, 1895, though, a former professional pitcher, Charles "Pacer" Smith, was hanged for the murder of his daughter and sister-in-law—a bloody act that shocked the Illinois town of Decatur.

Charles N. Smith was born in Pendleton, Indiana, on August 4, 1853. He was the fourth of the ten children of John and Rebecca Smith. John Smith was a shoemaker who joined the Union army shortly after the start of the Civil War. In late 1864, he was thrown from his horse and reportedly spent six months in a hospital. He never completely recovered from the injury; the *Decatur Daily Review* described him as "practically a cripple."

Family members described Charles as a very bright boy with a penchant for sports, although he never played professionally until he was twenty-three. He was always fond of sports, and as the game of baseball was just beginning to be popular during his early manhood, he naturally drifted into that profession. He had earned a good reputation as a pitcher, however, and was offered and accepted a position with the Cincinnati Red Stockings.

Smith started his professional career in the mid-1870s. Although he was the property of the Cincinnati major-league team, he never appeared in a regular season major-league contest. His playing time was apparently confined to exhibition games (which were frequent during those seasons) and action with area independent teams. Even so, Smith's play in Cincinnati was enough to get him noticed, and he spent the next few seasons in cities that would later have major-league or strong minor-league teams. He played for the Baltimore Blues in 1878 and 1879 and for Nashville in 1880. He then returned to Indiana, spending 1881 with Terre Haute and the next two seasons with Indianapolis, both of the Northwestern League. Though he was not retained when Indianapolis got major-league baseball in 1884, Smith stayed in the area with the Noblesville team that year. In 1885, he played for clubs in Jacksonville, Florida, and Greencastle and Evansville, Indiana.

During the early 1880s, John and Rebecca Smith separated, though they apparently remained married. Rebecca Smith and three of her children moved west to Illinois. Settling first in Danville and Mattoon, they eventually moved to the Decatur area. Initially, Charles lived with a married sister in Indianapolis, but in 1886 he moved to Decatur to pitch for the local team.

When Smith was recruited to come to Decatur in the late 1880s, the city's once-outstanding professional baseball team, the Yellow Hammers, was foundering at the bottom of its division. "Pacer" Smith was known for his

Charles "Pacer" Smith in an illustration during his heyday as a professional baseball player. *Decatur Evening Bulletin.*

infamous fastball and style on the ball field. He was lured to Decatur in hopes that he could revive the ailing team, but no one had any idea that his residency in the city would end in horrible tragedy and murder.

Smith managed to revive the dreadful Yellow Hammers during the 1887 season and became quite popular around town, especially with the ladies. He was a smooth talker, a flashy dresser, widely traveled and famous for his curling, handlebar mustache. He also became known for his drinking and could often be found, when not on the baseball field, in one of the local taverns.

In 1888, Smith married one of his female fans, a young Decatur woman named Maggie Buchert. Unfortunately, that year brought bad news to Smith when the Yellow Hammers disbanded. He began searching for work, and his drinking became worse. Over the next several years, Smith played for baseball clubs in cities all over Illinois, including Champaign, Bloomington, Ottawa and Shreveport. He made several attempts to get back into the larger leagues, but his once lightning-fast pitching had slowed down, and rumors began to spread about his heavy drinking.

In 1890, Smith's wife, Maggie, became pregnant and gave birth to a baby girl named Louise. Soon after, Smith realized that married life was not to his liking, and his drinking became even worse. He spent little time at home, choosing to frequent the saloons when not traveling out of town to play baseball. By 1893, he was considered completely unreliable by the more reputable clubs, and he was forced to play baseball in Pana, Illinois, where he also served as a town policeman. After the end of the season, he was fired from both jobs and returned to look for work in Decatur. The once nationally known baseball player was soon working as a cook at the Hoffman House, and other Franklin and Park Streets taverns, setting out free lunches for drinking men. It was a long fall from the fame that he once enjoyed as a professional baseball player.

Smith's drinking and his increasing bitterness destroyed his marriage. Maggie finally decided to leave him and, with her daughter, moved back into her father's home at 758 East Lawrence Street. She told Smith that he was welcome to come and see Louise anytime that he liked, and while he never contributed any sort of support for his wife and daughter, he did visit on a fairly regular basis. The rest of his life continued to deteriorate. His drinking grew steadily worse, and eventually it would be alcohol that would ruin him for good.

On Saturday, September 28, 1895, Smith spent the entire day drinking in a saloon on South Park Street. He was a regular customer, so he had little trouble convincing the bartender to loan him his revolver. He left the tavern and went to the home of his father-in-law, Frank Buchert, where Maggie,

Louisa and Maggie's sister, Edna, also lived. When he arrived there, he asked for his daughter, but Louise was not there at the time. Edna offered to go and look for her, and she went off down the street, leaving Smith waiting on the front porch. Louise, who was six years old at the time, was playing with friends in a neighbor's yard, but Edna brought her back home to see her father. Witnesses later testified that Smith never gave any inclination that he was upset about anything—or that he planned to kill anyone.

The house where the Bucherts lived was a one-story structure with a high basement. When Edna returned with the child, they sat down on the steps together. Smith was standing nearby, and Maggie had also come out to visit. She was standing on the steps a few feet away. Then—suddenly and without any warning—Smith removed the borrowed revolver from his coat and fired at his daughter. The shot struck Louise in the neck, and she made a loud, choking cry as she pitched forward and rolled down the stairs to land at her father's feet. Maggie and Edna, utterly terrified, screamed and scrambled up the stairs and away from the gun. Smith fired a second shot at Maggie, and it narrowly missed her, lodging in the ceiling of the front porch. She began to scream for help, rushing away from the house and in the direction of Jacobs' Butcher Shop, where her father worked, a half block away.

The exact manner of Edna Buchert's murder will never be known, as Smith was the only witness and he never told. The only thing that can be stated for certain is that Smith turned his gun on her and fired one time. She was struck near the back door of the house, and she ran around to the east side of the house and fell dead on the front walk. Her father found her there, covered in blood, a short time later.

Maggie narrowly escaped the violence. She burst through the door of the butcher shop, screaming, "Charlie has shot Louise!" Frank Buchert immediately ran to his house, where he discovered Edna on the sidewalk. Buchert dropped to his knees and pulled Edna to him in a grief-stricken embrace. He called her name several times, but it was too late; the young woman was already dead. Buchert looked up and saw Charles Smith standing just a short distance away. He was coldly gazing at the scene, the smoking revolver still in his hand. Buchert pleaded with Smith to tell him why he had done such a terrible thing. Smith gave him an angry reply, "You be a little careful, or I'll give you your own dose of lead."

Buchert laid Edna's body carefully on the ground and, his hands crimson with his daughter's blood, ran to the fallen body of his granddaughter. Louise was unconscious but still alive, although she was bleeding badly. He picked her up and carried her into the house, gently placing her on a bed.

By this time, neighbors had started to gather, and one of the men carried Edna's body into the house and placed her on a lounge in the living room.

With one last glance at the Buchert house, "Pacer" Smith walked calmly and slowly down the street in the direction of the butcher shop, possibly looking for his wife. Luckily, he never found her.

A telephone call was made to the police headquarters from the Jacobs' store, and details were passed along about the crime, along with the identity of the murderer. Chief Mason and Officer Howard Williams jumped into a buggy and headed down Broadway (present-day Martin Luther King Boulevard) toward the Buchert home. Deputy Sheriff Frank Taylor and Officer Cross went down Webster Street in search of the killer. At Clay Street, they ran into Mr. Jacobs, Frank Buchert's employer, who had been following the killer. He told the officers that Smith had started walking north. Moments later, they saw Smith heading into a nearby alley, and both men jumped from the buggy and ran toward him, just in time to see him disappear into a yard. Both men drew their revolvers, expecting a fight, as they advanced on him.

As the officers rounded the corner of a house, they were surprised to see Smith walking toward them. He held the revolver in his right hand, and when Cross grabbed hold of him, he released it. He offered no resistance, and when Cross asked him why he had done it, his only reply was that he "had had lots of trouble and he had finally put an end to it all."

Chief Mason and Officer Williams arrived a few moments later and helped take Smith into custody. He was taken to the jail, and within thirty minutes after the murder, the killer was behind bars. Smith was charged with Edna Buchert's killing. He was charged with a second murder on Monday morning, when Louise died from her wound.

Word quickly spread through Decatur about the brutal murders—and about the famous killer. The excitement was intense, and lynching was freely spoken of on the streets and in the taverns and saloons. Even police officers were upset and angry over the crime. Officer Brockway, who was described as "one of the oldest and most reliable men on the police force," rushed at Smith when he was first brought to the jail and tried to attack him with his billy club. Other officers restrained him, but they did so reluctantly. Brockway was the uncle of Maggie and Edna Buchert, and only the cooler heads of the other officers kept him from killing Smith with his bare hands.

Shortly after Smith was locked up, he was interrogated by Sheriff I.P. Nicholson. On Saturday night, Smith refused to talk. His replies to the questions that Nicholson asked were disjointed and strange. Nicholson began, "What was the matter with you today, Pacer?"

"What have I done? I don't know what you mean," Smith replied.

Nicholson was incensed. "Don't attempt that. You haven't got sense enough to play crazy. You had better fess up and tell the whole story, and it will go better for you."

But Smith just shook his head and refused to explain the reasons behind what he had done. "I have had lots of trouble, but it's all over now. I'm sick now but will tell you all about it tomorrow."

The newspapers reported that Smith became sick that night, and his "entire faculties seemed to collapse." The police feared that he was being seized by delirium from

Sheriff I.P. Nicholson. *Decatur Evening Bulletin.*

alcohol (everyone was aware of his heavy drinking), but the next morning he seemed to rally, and his health improved. In spite of this, he never kept his promise to Sheriff Nicholson and refused to explain why he had shot Louise and Edna. In fact, his only regret over the course of the next few days was that he had been unable to kill his wife.

On Monday, following the death of Louise, a grand jury indicted Smith for both murders. That afternoon, he was taken into court and arraigned for trial. Attorneys Bunn and Park were appointed to defend him, but they asked to be excused, and I.A. Buckingham was appointed in their place. On Wednesday, Smith was brought into court, where he entered a guilty plea for the murder of Louise. However, he stated that he was not guilty of Edna's murder, apparently believing that since he meant to kill his wife, not his sister-in-law, he was less accountable for the brutal crime.

On Monday, October 8, Smith was brought back into court to have his sentence pronounced. After hearing evidence from a number of witnesses, Judge Vail asked Smith's attorney if he had a statement that he wanted to make on behalf of his client. Buckingham and Smith held a whispered conversation for a few moments, and then Smith stood and asked to speak. He spoke quietly in a calm voice that was almost impossible to hear. His voice faltered several times as he made his statement:

> *I borrowed the gun and went down there to kill the lady and the child—my wife. I understood that if I pled guilty that I would be hung and I am willing to do it, but would like to have it put off until the sixteenth of February. I am willing to face anybody and everybody.*

Smith then took his seat again and wiped the perspiration that had beaded on his forehead with a black silk handkerchief. The judge asked Buckingham if he had anything that he wanted to add, and the attorney stated that he didn't.

Judge Vail then spoke:

> *When a man pleads guilty to murder in the first degree as is charged in this indictment, he places himself at the discretion of the court to be sentenced, to be hanged or to be confined in the penitentiary for life or for a term not less than fourteen years. I can see that a man can be so injured, or so abused that his wrongs may so weigh upon him until he imagines that he is in a way justified in murder. But it is not apparent that there was any ill feeling in this family. I cannot imagine how any man could have any ill feeling or hold any hatred that would cause him to willfully take the life of a mere child. In my judgment, this is a case where justice demands the extreme penalty of the law, but it is not an easy task. The law is the highest exponent that teaches the duty of one citizen to another and no man has the right to take the law into his own hands. Now, if Mr. Smith has anything to say in extenuating him from this crime, then I want to hear it.*

Smith only shook his head. He would never speak about why he had committed the murders.

The judge then ordered Smith to stand as he passed sentence: "It is the sentence of this court that you be taken back to the Macon County jail, and there be securely confined, until the twenty-ninth day of November, when you shall be taken out and hanged by the neck until dead."

During the pronouncement of the sentence, Smith stared silently at the judge. He stood completely still, a blank expression on his face. It was not until the judge was finished that color came back into his face. He slumped in what seemed to be relief, bowed his head and whispered, "Thank you."

The silence of the courtroom was shattered, though, by the piercing tones of a woman's voice. A murmur of approval rippled through the courtroom as Maggie Smith cried out, "Thank God, he has got his just dues. My baby, oh, my baby!" Many of those in attendance that day later stated that they would never forget her words, or the crushing grief that could be heard in her voice.

Maggie then burst into tears and was comforted by several friends. Frank Buchert, who was next to her, sprang from his seat and, turning to the crowd, said, "That is all I want; the law will give him what he deserves."

Smith was hustled out of the courtroom, and the crowd parted as he walked out between Sheriff Nicholson and Deputy Holmes. As he passed a group of his friends from the taverns, he made the motion of putting a rope around his neck and pretended to pull it tight. He laughed, "The twenty-ninth of November, boys."

When he was outside, he told the sheriff that he was perfectly happy with the sentence and had only feared that he would be given a life sentence in the penitentiary instead. He never explained why he had asked for the hanging to be delayed until February.

Smith was removed from his common cell at the jail that afternoon and taken to a solitary cell in the upstairs portion of the building. The following afternoon, he was visited by Father Charles Brady, the assistant pastor of St. Patrick's Church. The young priest spoke to Smith at length about his spiritual welfare. Father Brady returned several times over the course of the next few days, and a week later, Smith was baptized into the Roman Catholic Church. Smith seemed to feel a great deal better after the service, and the newspapers reported, "Despite what may be said to the contrary, Smith ever after his baptism seemed to feel better and bore up under the ordeal of awaiting his last day with remarkable fortitude."

Smith remained incarcerated in his solitary cell, until, about two weeks before his execution, he was placed on "death watch," which meant that he was constantly under guard. Deputy Sam Stabler performed the duty during the daytime, and Tom Richardson stayed with Smith at night. Smith grew especially fond of Stabler and often spoke of him to reporters. Shortly before his death, he told one newspaper reporter:

> *The sheriff has been just as kind to me as I could wish. Anything I want, I get. A man could not treat a guest better than Sheriff Nicholson does me. Sam Stabler is all right, too. He is the same old fellow every day and we get along all right.*

Thursday, November 28, was Smith's last Thanksgiving. He was in good spirits, visited with his priest and his family and ate a hearty dinner of turkey with oyster dressing, gravy, sweet and Irish potatoes, a piece of pie and a large glass of milk. His father, mother, brothers and several sisters stayed with him in his cell for several hours, but when his mother started to leave, she collapsed with grief and had to be escorted out by the officers on duty. About 3:00 p.m., Smith's brother J.E. Smith went to the Buchert home and tried to convince Maggie and Frank Buchert to come to the jail and see Smith one last time. Both of them refused. Father Brady stayed with Smith throughout the remainder of the day and promised to return the next morning with Father Higgins of Taylorville to give Smith communion one last time.

Smith rose early on the morning of Friday, November 29. He ate breakfast and then took a short nap in his cell. He told reporters that he did this so that he would feel better about his ordeal at noon. One of the reporters asked him if he had heard about a reprieve that had recently been granted to another prisoner, and Smith said that he had, noting that the man's death sentence had been commuted after he became a Christian and was baptized. Smith had written a letter to the man, and he claimed this had been the key to the prisoner's religious conversion. When Smith was asked what he would say to a reprieve for himself, he snapped his fingers and said, "I don't care that much. I am all ready to go."

Just before noon, Sheriff Nicholson came to Smith's cell and read aloud his death warrant. Father Brady and Father Higgins stood nearby, and Smith listened calmly. The sheriff led the procession to the jail yard, where a scaffold stood. Hundreds of people from Decatur came to see the gallows on Thursday afternoon, streaming in and out of the yard to see the "infernal device" that would claim Smith's life. On the day of the execution, only about three hundred ticket holders were allowed to witness the hanging.

As the procession climbed the stairs, reporters noted that Smith was "pale but determined." The two priests prayed with him a final time, and then the hood and the noose were slipped over his head. Under the platform, three doctors waited to pronounce Smith dead. A few moments later, Smith plunged to his doom.

It was obvious to everyone who knew him in his final days that "Pacer" Smith wanted to die for the crimes that he had committed. He would never speak of what had led him to commit the brutal crime of shooting his own child and trying to murder his wife and killing his sister-in-law instead. Whatever drove him to it, he seemed to believe that death was the only thing that would ease his conscience and assuage his guilt.

The Body on the Railroad Tracks

Until the minute the coroner arrived on the scene, the engineer of the Joliet & Eastern freight train was sure that he had killed the woman who was sprawled in a tangled, bloody heap alongside the railroad tracks. His locomotive had struck her as it cut through the darkness underneath a viaduct a half-mile north of Wayne, Illinois. The time was 8:22 p.m. on Friday, September 26, 1913.

The story of this mysterious woman would create a sensation in Northern Illinois and would involve dance halls, ex-husbands, a prison convict and as many as two dozen murdered young women.

Du Page County Coroner Hopf and Sheriff Kuhn were soon on the scene of what seemed to be a railroad accident. After Hopf had examined the body, he made an announcement that, although reassuring to the train's engineer, was ominous to the sheriff. "This woman was dead for a half hour when the train hit her. She was shot through the head. Obviously, the body was placed on the tracks to simulate an accident."

Even in the light of the investigator's lanterns, and after being struck by the locomotive, the features of the dead woman gave evidence that in life, she had been more than ordinarily attractive. She was auburn haired and looked to be about thirty-five years old. She wore a smart blue suit, white gloves and expensive red shoes. Near the body was a red purse that Kuhn searched to see if he could find any clue to her identity. It contained a handkerchief, face powder, a comb and a visiting card that was engraved with the name "Mildred Allison." A small change purse held a few coins but no bills.

The fact that Mildred Allison was the woman's name seemed to be corroborated by the gold bracelet on her left wrist. It bore the inscription "W.H.A. to M.A." However, another discovery on the rail bed offered conflicting information. The sheriff found a letter, torn into several pieces, which the investigators were able to reconstruct well enough to learn that the salutation read, "Dear Mrs. Rexroat." Aside from its proximity to the body, there was nothing to suggest that the letter was connected to the victim. Nevertheless, the police collected the fragments for further study.

The body was taken to the morgue, and then Sheriff Kuhn began to make local inquiries about the victim. Soon, newspaper reporters from Chicago, about thirty miles to the east, got wind of the story, and details began appearing in their daily publications. By midmorning of the following day, the agent at the Wayne station of the Aurora, Elgin & Chicago interurban electric railroad had contacted the police. He was certain that he had seen the dead woman before.

The rail agent told the police that on the night of September 26, the woman, carrying a small rattan suitcase, had gotten off the 7:25 p.m. train from Chicago. A man whom the agent described as wearing glasses,

Illustration of the woman leaving the train with the rattan suitcase. *Illustration by Glenn Grohe.*

of medium height, clean-shaven, wavy haired and carefully dressed accompanied her. The two had left the Elgin station and headed toward the nearby tracks of the Joliet & Eastern. An hour later, the man returned alone. He was now carrying the rattan suitcase. Before he boarded the 8:30 p.m. Chicago-bound Elgin train, he presented a return ticket to Chicago for a refund.

When the sheriff completed the restoration of the letter fragments, he realized that, if connected to the victim, the note indicated her occupation. The message—dated September 23 and signed by John Zook—appeared to be a reply to Mrs. Rexroat concerning the rental of a hall for dance classes. Zook had informed his correspondent that the hall could be engaged for ten dollars per night, including light, heat and janitor service. The envelope in which the letter was mailed could not be found, and Zook's address was not on the single sheet of reconstructed paper.

While Kuhn was pondering the whereabouts of Zook—for there was no one by that name in the area around Wayne—a report came in that strengthened the supposition that the victim had been a dancer and, in turn, the likely recipient of the letter. A discovery had been made by a trackwalker for the Elgin rail line early that morning when he stumbled across a pink dancing gown and a pair of pink slippers. The garments, which were in fresh condition, were the exact size of the victim. They had been found on the right side of the rail bed, suggesting that they had been tossed from a Chicago-bound train.

At noon, John J. Halpin, a Chicago chief of detectives, telephoned Kuhn and told him that a man named William H. Allison had just come into headquarters and stated that he was afraid the dead woman might be his former wife. Allison told Halpin that he had once given her a bracelet that matched the description of the one the dead woman was wearing. Allison asked if the body could be moved to Chicago so that he could take charge of the funeral arrangements.

Kuhn agreed but told Halpin that he was taking the first train to Chicago to talk with Allison himself. Detective Halpin set up an interview room, where William Allison tearfully identified the dead woman as his former wife, Mildred. He told a sad story of their marriage. The two had married seventeen years before, when Mildred was eighteen years old. For some time, they got along well, but several years before, Mildred had started frequenting dance halls, cafés and other nightspots. Eventually, this brought an end to their marriage. They lived apart for months, and then in May 1913 they divorced. Allison claimed that he had had no contact with Mildred since that time and only knew that she had been living in the home of friends, Mr. and Mrs. Victor Johnson, on Eggleston Avenue in Chicago. He was also aware that she had become a dance teacher.

As for the puzzling salutation of "Mrs. Rexroat" and the identity of Zook, Allison declared that he was completely in the dark. He also knew of no one who might have any reason to want to kill his ex-wife, although, as the officers who heard the story also realized, there had been a number of men in her life.

The Rexroat angle of the story was solved after a visit to the Johnson house. Here, Kuhn and Halpin interviewed Mrs. Johnson, who confirmed Mildred's residence with the family and provided additional information about Mildred's life, including the fact that William Allison had not been her last husband. After their divorce, she had married a farmer from Macomb named Everett Rexroat. However, the month before, Mildred had left her second husband and had come to live with the Johnsons. At present, she had taken a job as a dance instructor at the Club Felicia in the Chicago Loop.

The officers obtained a description of Everett Rexroat from Mrs. Johnson and realized that, in general, it fit the man who had been seen with Mildred in Wayne. The only exception was that Rexroat did not wear eyeglasses.

Mrs. Johnson described the last time that she had seen her friend:

> *Mildred left the house late yesterday afternoon. Earlier, she got a phone call. The connection was bad and she became impatient. She handed the phone to me and said, "See if you can figure out what he's talking about." I took the call. It was a man who wanted Mildred to meet him in time to catch the 6:28 to Wayne, where he had a dancing class for her all arranged. No, he didn't tell me his name, although, of course, Mildred seemed to know who it was.*

Mrs. Johnson added that she did not know a John Zook, but she did recall Mildred leaving the house carrying a rattan suitcase the day before. She also remembered her wearing a large diamond ring that had been a gift from Everett Rexroat. The ring had not been found with her body. This piece of information, combined with the fact that no money had been found in her purse, suggested that Mildred had been killed during a robbery. Apparently, the police thought, the killer had lured her to a deserted spot on the railroad tracks under the pretext of having arranged a dance class in Wayne.

Kuhn and Halpin left the Johnson home and returned to police headquarters, where they immediately put a call through to the sheriff's office in McDonough County, of which Macomb—about two hundred miles southwest of Chicago—was the county seat. They asked that Rexroat be informed of his wife's death and, if he was in Macomb, that he be escorted to Chicago.

Then, Kuhn and Halpin went to Club Felicia. The nightspot, a publicly patronized dance hall, was well into the swing of its evening activity. The owner acknowledged Mildred's recent employment there but stated that he didn't know her very well and knew nothing of her habits, friends or outside activities. He did recall, though, that there had been one man who had been in lately who seemed to monopolize all of her time. The owner didn't know his name but described him as being a "natty dresser," having wavy hair and wearing eyeglasses.

It was almost the exact same description of the mysterious man who had been seen by the railroad agent on the night that Mildred had been killed.

On the afternoon of Sunday, September 28, Everett Rexroat arrived in Chicago. When asked to identify the body of his wife, he complied, but when he did so, he showed little emotion. Halpin noticed his lack of grief and asked him about it.

Rexroat replied, "You think it odd? Well, maybe you'd change your mind if you knew what our life together was like."

He explained that he had met Mildred in October 1912, when he came to Chicago to study the garage business. He fell in love with her and, soon after the New Year, asked her to marry him. He'd been shocked when she told him that she was already married. However, she explained that she had not been living with her husband and agreed to seek a divorce. After she obtained it, they were married, on May 26 in Crown Point, Indiana. Until July 31, they had lived in Chicago, and then Rexroat's father wrote to him and told him that help was needed on the family farm. He asked that he and his new wife come back to live in Macomb. Farm life appalled Mildred, and soon after they arrived, she made it very clear that she missed the lights of Chicago. She couldn't wait to get back to them, she often told her husband.

The incident that finally precipitated her departure involved an itinerant photographer who stopped by the farm to take pictures. After he left, Mildred expressed great admiration for him and compared his "ginger" to the "louts" around her. The next day, August 26, she left Macomb and never returned. Rexroat stated that he had heard nothing from her since that time, although he did receive a letter from a man who represented himself as a Chicago attorney declaring that Mildred was in a maternity hospital and demanding money for her care. Rexroat had ignored the letter and, later, destroyed it, recognizing it as an attempt to perpetrate a fraud.

Kuhn asked him if the name "Zook" meant anything to him, and Rexroat recognized it right away. "He lives in Bushnell, fifteen miles from Macomb, and owns a lot of real estate, including a hall which he rents out," he said. "Mildred met him while she was living on the farm and thought, I guess, the hall would be a good place to give dance lessons."

Rexroat admitted to giving Mildred the diamond ring and told Halpin that he had paid $350 for it. Halpin asked him where he had been on the night of his wife's murder, and he said that he had been playing cards with several friends, whom he named, in Macomb.

Halpin asked if he had been around the Club Felicia lately, and Rexroat claimed that he had never heard of the place. When it was explained that his wife had been working there, he seemed puzzled. He said, "When she left Macomb, she told me that she was going back to work at Sans Souci Park. That's where I first met her."

Halpin started two inquiries in McDonough County through its local officers; first, to look into Rexroat's alibi, and next, to talk with John Zook. Both of these tasks turned out to be unnecessary after Halpin and Kuhn paid a visit to Sans Souci Park. They learned that Mildred had worked in the dance hall during the 1912 season and had returned for the last few days of August 1913. On these last occasions, she had often been accompanied by a wavy-haired man who wore eyeglasses. She had introduced him to several of the other girls who worked there.

Halpin asked one of the dancers, "What was his name?"

"Henry Spencer," she replied.

Ironically, Detective Halpin knew exactly who Henry Spencer was, and in fact, the man had come to him just a few weeks before looking for help in finding a job. Spencer was on parole from Joliet Prison for robbery, and Halpin had assisted him in finding some employment, but the ex-convict didn't last at the position for long.

With this new information, Halpin and Kuhn rushed back to police headquarters and obtained Spencer's file. The man had been in and out of Illinois jails since his youth, and a frequently recurring charge was for molestation of women and fraud. Within hours, those who had seen Mildred's companion at Club Felicia, Sans Souci Park and the Wayne train station positively identified Spencer's photograph as the man they had seen.

Now that the investigators knew the identity of the man last seen with Mildred, they had to find him. In Spencer's file, it noted that he had lived for a time with a woman who occupied an apartment on Michigan Avenue, so

Halpin and Kuhn called on her. They found her to be surprisingly cooperative but quickly understood why when she went on for several minutes about Spencer's faithless ways and the inconsiderate manner in which he treated her. Hell hath no fury, the investigators knew, like a woman scorned.

She reported that she had last seen Spencer the previous Friday night, when he had been very anxious and nervous. She recalled that he had come to her apartment with a small rattan suitcase, from which, in her presence, he had removed a single shell from a revolver and had thrown it out the window.

Halpin, now certain that Spencer was the killer, ordered the woman to say nothing of their visit and set up an around-the-clock detail to keep watch on the apartment. For six days, this surveillance yielded nothing, but then, on Saturday, October 4, Spencer was arrested as he walked into his girlfriend's building.

At police headquarters, he first denied any knowledge of Mildred Allison and claimed that he knew nothing about her death. When he realized the strength of the case against him, though, he changed his story and offered a full confession—and then some.

According to Spencer, he had met Mildred at Sans Souci Park. The two of them began telling each other their troubles and a relationship started, although Spencer said that he always thought of Mildred as "easy pickings." He told the investigators:

> *The day I killed her, she met me at the Aurora & Elgin station. We bought tickets to Wayne and on the way out, we talked about our love affair. We were to be married. After I killed her, I caught a train back to Chicago and threw her dancing clothes out the window. I kept the suitcase and gave the ring to another girl.*

Spencer freely admitted that he had murdered Mildred Allison but then went on to shock the detectives by telling them that he had also killed two dozen other women in Illinois and the Midwest. It was subsequently proven that much of this "confession" was sheer imagination, but it was also probable that he told the truth in describing his responsibility for at least six of these murders.

One consistent thread ran through his revelations: an almost maniacal hatred of women. He told Detective Halpin:

> *Sometimes you can trust a living man—never a living woman. I hate them all—all of them. It seems as if I could look into their lying little brains*

and watch them scheming against me. So, I pat them on the cheek, call them sweet names—and kill them.

Although prosecutors had a number of charges for which to try Spencer, they chose his last, and perhaps his most coldblooded: the murder of Mildred Allison Rexroat. On November 14, 1913, in the Du Page County Courthouse at Wheaton, Henry Spencer was found guilty and sentenced to hang. The court's pronouncement was carried out on July 31, 1914.

Red Lights on the Prairie

It was not uncommon to find brothels and houses of prostitution scattered across the prairies of Northern Illinois, but the city of Decatur stood far above the rest when it came to the sheer numbers of disorderly houses, crime areas and a segregated red-light district that remained in existence until 1936. It was an unusually corrupt city government that made such crime possible in Decatur and allowed the existence of several vice areas, including the notorious Levee District on the city's east side. There, just steps away from Decatur's two train stations, locals and visitors alike could find every manner of vice imaginable, from liquor to gambling.

Prostitution had arrived in Decatur with the railroads. There may have been a few disorderly houses, as brothels were commonly referred to, in existence in Decatur prior to the late 1850s, but they didn't make news until after the start of the Civil War. Like the formation of the Levee District to serve the entertainment needs of visiting soldiers, sporting houses were created because of demand. By the late 1800s, a segregated red-light district had been established in the 500 and 600 blocks of East William Street, and the sporting houses were mostly left alone to operate there. Occasionally, a raid would take place at one establishment or another—usually because protection payments had fallen behind—but most of those raids occurred outside the boundaries of the red-light district, which was a short two blocks away from the Levee.

Although never segregated like the red-light district on East William Street, other sections of town played host to brothels, especially on the South Side. Neighborhoods along South Main Street were known for their disorderly houses. One such district on the South Side of town was known as "Oklahoma." The area took its name in the late 1800s, when the Oklahoma Territory was opening out West and land was being given away to anyone who wanted it. A down-on-his-luck man from Decatur made plans to travel out to Oklahoma and stake his claim, but his broken-down wagon only made it as far as the South Side of the city before the axle broke and his trip was cut short. With no other prospects, he simply pitched a tent next to the wagon and made it his home. His friends needled him about moving to "Oklahoma," and the name stuck.

A neighborhood of sorts grew up around the luckless pioneer, and soon others with no work and no money came to the area. The land there was so cheap that almost anyone could afford it. Lots were sold for as little as three dollars, and not surprisingly, this did not attract the best housing. Many who lived there resided in tents, wagons and hastily thrown-together shacks.

Lawlessness abounded in this region, along with squalid living conditions. There were no real waste disposal systems to speak of, and hog pens located near the river drained directly into the city's water supply. In 1916, the area was annexed to the city, but there was little officials could do about the horrible conditions. Eventually, most of Oklahoma was wiped out when Lake Decatur was formed. The damming of the river flooded out the worst areas, but many of the residents simply relocated to the other side of Main Street.

There, on the north side of Greenwood Cemetery, was a district that was dubbed "Coaltown." This area was named thanks to the fact that most of the residents worked in the Decatur coal mines. Living conditions there were only slightly better than those in Oklahoma. It was still a collection of shacks, shanties and "shotgun houses" (rooms built in a line, one after another, so called because a shotgun could be fired through the front door and the shell would exit out the back door). It was essentially an area without law. In addition to rampant prostitution, other vices like illegal liquor and gambling could also be found there. Coaltown lasted into the 1940s, when it was finally demolished.

Prostitution made good copy in the newspapers of the past, often shocking the more conservative residents of Decatur, who pretended not to know that the sex trade was operating in their midst. Some of the local prostitutes and madams, like a streetwalker named "Sweet Sarah," whose exploits appeared almost weekly in Decatur newspapers during the early 1900s, and disorderly house owners like "Red Ethel," became local characters.

On April 28, 1888, a young woman named Mollie Miller was arrested and confessed to keeping a house of ill repute on East Main Street in a home owned by Mrs. Elizabeth Davis. The newspaper editor commented:

Red Lights on the Prairie

*The closing up of that den of temptation is a source of some great gratification
to all decent people, especially those dwelling in that neighborhood and all
who are compelled to pass by that house. There are several other dens in and
out of the city that should also be closed up.*

Occasionally, neighbors of sporting houses complained to the police and managed to get them closed down. In February 1895, a woman named Katherine Hamilton swore out a warrant against the owner of a house down the street from where she lived. She went before the state's attorney and charged Eva Vahler with harboring an underage girl, Hettie Mercer, in a house of prostitution. Vahler was arrested, and Hettie, who had voluntarily gone to work as a prostitute, was returned to her parents.

In June 1895, Captain Holmes and Officers Bailey and Dempsey raided a bawdyhouse on South Main Street that was kept by a woman named Ruby Dawson. Four prostitutes were captured and taken to the city jail for the night. Police also raided a house on Merchant Street and arrested four more women. The keepers of the houses were fined twenty-five dollars each, and the prostitutes each had to surrender ten dollars.

"Last night, Captain Muthersbaugh and several officers made a hasty march on the Lou Johnson disreputable resort south of the city and captured several fallen angels," the newspapers reported in February 1896. A number of men who were "keeping company" with the ladies were also arrested, and the entire crowd was brought back to the police station and fined.

"Oh, what's the use of living anyway?" Orvis Cordray asked in 1905, citing despair as the reason that he tried to kill himself at the St. James Hotel on the morning of August 5.

Cordray was a twenty-one-year-old man from Portland, Indiana, who began working in Decatur at the Walrus Manufacturing Company. Before coming to Decatur, he had lived in Shelbyville for a time and, while there, married a young woman by the name of Marie Benning. When he came to Decatur, he brought his new bride with him, but after a few days together, Marie left him and took up residence at a house of ill repute on South Park Street. Things were quiet for a few days, but then Cordray began to brood about his wife's actions. He wanted her to give up her life as a prostitute and come back to live with him, but she refused. On August 4, he returned to the sporting house and begged her to return to him. Marie sent him away again, and this time he left with the intention of ending his troubles with a bullet.

The next morning, Cordray went into work and told his employers that he planned to return to Indiana; he asked for all of the money that he had coming to him. He then took the money and went to Sam Berstein's secondhand store at the corner of Eldorado and Broadway and purchased an Ivers & Johnson .22-caliber revolver. Armed with it, he returned to the St. James Hotel, where he and Marie had been staying together. He had every intention of killing himself when he went into the bathroom. He sat down on the edge of the tub and placed the revolver to his chest, hoping that the bullet would pierce his heart. He pulled the trigger, and the shot was heard by Mrs. Corley, the wife of the hotel's owner. She notified her husband at once and then raced to the bathroom, where she found Cordray sprawled out on the floor with the smoking pistol still in his hand. Her husband took away the gun and then raised Cordray into a sitting position. He was still breathing and asked for a doctor. When the physician arrived, the first thing that the young man asked him was whether the wound would be fatal. The doctor replied that there was no way to tell just yet, bandaged the wound and had the man transported to St. Mary's Hospital. When he arrived there, he was examined, and the bullet was found to have missed his heart; it had passed through the edge of his lung and lodged in the muscle of his upper back. He was expected to recover, but an operation would be needed to retrieve the bullet once the young man recovered his strength. Cordray expressed regret over trying to kill himself.

On August 16, Cordray's doctors went to the hospital to prepare for surgery to remove the bullet. However, when they arrived, one of the sisters on duty informed them that Cordray had jumped out of a window that morning and fled the hospital. Some of the orderlies had searched for him, but he was nowhere to be found. Orvis Cordray was never seen in Decatur again.

In the early 1900s, stories of white slavery were prominent in news reports and in the lurid bestsellers that were penned by well-meaning reformers intent on doing away with prostitution and houses of ill repute. Many news stories cited cases of young women who were pressed into service as prostitutes and who did not willingly go to work in brothels. Once such case occurred in Decatur in February 1910, and the police learned of it after receiving a report about a drunken nude girl walking down North Water Street. The twenty-one-year-old girl's name was Viola Harris, and she was first seen at the Gushard store about 7:00 p.m. on Sunday, February 20. Followed by a number of jeering men, she stumbled into the store clad only in her chemise and stockings, apparently so intoxicated that she could barely stand. Shocked at the behavior of the people on the sidewalk, one of the store clerks opened an umbrella and shielded the girl from view until Officer

Powell arrived. He took the girl to the Moran undertaking establishment, where she was given a blanket to cover herself. The crowd that had followed her was still milling about on the sidewalk when Viola was transported to police headquarters.

Viola had been staying in rooms rented by Peter Harris above a tavern called the Bizzy Izzy on North Park Street. The second and third floors of the building were used as a house of ill repute. Viola was the sister of Mrs. W.W. Kish, who lived on South Colfax Street, and Mrs. Kish told the police that Viola had been at a home for delinquent girls in Claremont, Indiana, since she was nine years old. She had moved to Decatur just three months before to live with her sister and brother-in-law and work at a restaurant they owned. On Saturday night, Viola had telephoned to say that she would not be home that night, and before Mrs. Kish could reply, the receiver was hung up. Mrs. Kish made a search for her sister that night and again on Sunday morning.

After the girl was taken into police custody, Mrs. Kish and Officer Al Petty went to the brothel that was run by Peter Harris. Mrs. Kish told Harris that she knew the girl had been there and demanded the return of Viola's clothing. Harris at first denied any knowledge of Viola but later admitted that she had been there. However, he said that she had been drinking heavily and that any actions she had engaged in were of her own volition. He surrendered the girl's dress, and Officer Petty placed him under arrest. After doctors examined Viola, they realized that the young woman had been drugged and given liquor and had been ill used by a large number of men who visited Harris's rooms. Mrs. Kish swore out a warrant against Harris for disorderly conduct, keeping a place for immoral purposes and enticing a woman into his place for immoral purposes. Harris paid a bond of $100 for his appearance in Judge Wadell's court the following Friday and was released. He quickly skipped town and was never captured.

Viola Harris took quite some time to recover from her ordeal. She remained unconscious for three days in the medical ward of the jail and eventually had to be placed in a straitjacket to prevent her from pulling out her own hair. When she finally awakened, she managed to drink a cup of water and told her sister that, to her knowledge, she had not been drinking on Saturday night. She said that she met Harris while working at the restaurant on South Park Street. Doctors believed that Harris gave her some sort of "knock-out drops" and managed to get her into the bordello. Viola slowly recovered from the terrifying experience and went on to lead a normal life.

Prostitution arrests and sporting house raids continued in the 1910s and 1920s, almost always avoiding the segregated area on East William Street.

The Tucker House, a brothel located at 545 East William Street, the heart of Decatur's red-light district.

Raids that resulted in the arrests of dozens of people occurred, closing down bawdyhouses that managed to reopen again a few days later. In 1929, thirty-seven inmates and customers were arrested during two raids on houses on South Jackson and East Orchard Streets. Five days later, in September 1929, six more people were arrested when the police shut down sporting houses on North Water and North Morgan Streets. Two days later, five more people were picked up during a raid in the 700 block of East Eldorado. Raids continued into the early 1930s, and more fines were given out, houses were temporarily shuttered and names were printed in the newspapers, to the embarrassment of the men who frequented Decatur's brothels.

Despite attempts to clean up the city, the red-light district continued to thrive. It lasted until 1936, and when it was finally closed down, it was a major event. On the morning of March 14, newspapers reported the death of a local stockbroker named John King, who had been shot to death on the front porch of a brothel that was located at 545 East William Street, in the heart of the red-light district. The shooting, and the publicity that surrounded it, turned out to be the catalyst that closed down the segregated area for good.

Kenneth Ogbin, a guest at the brothel who was a former tavern owner and an unsuccessful Republican candidate for Macon County sheriff in 1934, admitted to shooting King but claimed that it was an accident. Late on Saturday evening, Ogbin was sleeping and was awakened by the owner of the brothel, Alice Hutchings (aka Alice Tucker). She told him that two men were on the front porch shouting and pounding on the door, demanding to be let in. Ogbin took his .38-caliber revolver and went downstairs to tell the men that they needed to leave. He opened the door, and King tried to push his way inside. Ogbin tried to push King back, shoving the barrel of his gun into the other man's abdomen. He then claimed that it accidentally went off. Ogbin fled from the house and, a few hours later, threw the gun into the lake. Later in the morning, he turned himself in when he heard that the police were looking for him. He had consulted with attorney L.E. Stephenson, who convinced him that this would be the right course of action.

John King, a forty-three-year-old stockbroker, was married and had a son in junior high school. King had offices in Decatur but had previously worked out of an office in the Wrigley Building in Chicago. In 1929, he lost most of his money in the stock market crash and moved to Decatur to work for Allen, Wiley & Jostes, an insurance and investment business. His father was Dr. John King, chief of staff of St. John's Hospital in Springfield. On the night he was shot, King and a drinking companion named L.A. Lynch decided to end their night by paying a visit to one of the local whorehouses. They first went to a house operated by Della Smull, but when they were refused admittance, they went down the street to a house owned by Alice Tucker. Both men were very drunk, and they began to pound and kick the door when Tucker refused to let them inside. Tucker then stated that she went to an upstairs room where Ogbin was sleeping. It was believed that Ogbin was living in the house free of charge in exchange for working as Tucker's security man. Ogbin was well known in town. In addition to once running for the office of sheriff, he also once owned a tavern on East Eldorado Street. Alice Tucker had worked for him in his saloon before becoming the owner of the sporting house.

An ambulance was called to transport King to St. Mary's Hospital, where he was found to be in critical condition. Tucker was arrested, as were Betty Thompson and Joyce Cook, two prostitutes who worked for her. After Ogbin surrendered to the police, he was charged in the shooting and then with murder when King died from his wounds.

Kenneth Ogbin was arrested for King's assault and murder.

Alice Hutchings (aka Alice Tucker), keeper of the brothel where King was killed.

The shooting was followed by a series of raids on houses in the red-light district, on North Broadway and at the Central Hotel at 528 North Water Street. Police Chief H.J. Schepper and city attorney S. Everett Wilson announced a deadline of Monday morning for all of the brothels to be emptied. Any of the operators or prostitutes still on the premises, or even still in the city of Decatur, would be fined and arrested. According to newspaper reports, the brothels were abandoned by Sunday night.

Dozens of women, and embarrassed male clients, were arrested in the raids. The prostitutes were warned that should they be caught in Decatur again, they would be charged with vagrancy and sentenced to at least six months in jail.

The raids in the wake of the John King murder effectively ended the segregated red-light district in Decatur. Today, nothing of the district remains. All of the houses that once stood on East William Street have been torn down and replaced by parking for newer buildings and empty weed-infested lots. A period of Decatur's history has been completely erased and all but forgotten by those who vaguely remember the days when Decatur was still a "wide-open" town.

Illinois Gangsters

The Saga of the Shelton Brothers

In a state like Illinois, which was often controlled by guns and violence, there were few men as fearsome as the Shelton brothers. From the Prohibition years, when they battled with the Ku Klux Klan and went to war with former ally Charlie Birger, to the days when they ran massive vice operations in Peoria and Northern Illinois, the Sheltons became widely known as men no one dared to cross.

KU KLUX KLAN IN ILLINOIS

When Prohibition came to Illinois in 1920, it turned many people into bootleggers. People wanted to drink, and there were those who offered to provide a service—in exchange for money, of course. With the liquor stills and illegal booze shipments came lawlessness, violence and bloodshed. Many in the region, especially in Southern Illinois, believed that they needed more help than local law enforcement could provide and welcomed the arrival of the Ku Klux Klan in 1923.

The Klan, a secret society that was organized in the South after the Civil War to reassert white supremacy, was resurrected with new vigor in the twentieth century, starting in Georgia in 1915. Although the original Ku Klux Klan accepted any white man, the new version excluded all but native-born Protestants and made clear the organization's distaste for immigrants, Catholics, Jews and, of course, blacks. Membership surged with the onset of Prohibition, and by the mid-1920s, membership had peaked at as many as five million men, some of whom were well-placed public officials.

The Klan vowed to clean up Southern Illinois, and at the head of the reform movement was a man named S. Glenn Young. Young was in his mid-thirties when he came to Illinois. He was raised in Kansas near the town of Long Island. His father was a rancher, and Young grew up with a gun in his hand. He was said to be a "dead shot" with a love for violence. At the age of twenty-one, he joined up with the Texas Rangers and spent most of his time hunting down cattle rustlers. He also served a two-year stint as a deputy United States marshal in Oklahoma. His early claim to fame came during World War I, when Young, working as an agent for the Bureau of Investigation in the Justice Department, brought in hundreds of draft dodgers and army deserters who were hiding out in the southern states. Young often traced these individuals alone, and many times they did not surrender without a fight. In October 1918, during a battle with deserters,

Prohibition and Ku Klux Klan agent S. Glenn Young. *Illinois State Historical Library.*

he reportedly killed at least one of the fugitives. Even after the war was over, Young was still tracking down what his biographer stated were murderous gangs in the Blue Ridge Mountains and other remote areas of the South.

In 1920, Young managed an appointment as a special agent in the Treasury Department's new Prohibition Unit, designed to enforce the Volstead Act. Assigned to Southern Illinois, he soon gained a reputation as a rough but successful operative. Before the end of the year, he was already in trouble. During a raid in a house with a still in Madison, located near East St. Louis, he shot and killed a man living next door to the house that was raided. The victim tried to shoot Young first, but his pistol misfired and Young gunned him down. Young was exonerated by a coroner's jury but was indicted by a Madison County grand jury. Since he was a federal officer, he was tried in federal court in Springfield. He was found not guilty on all charges in June 1921. In spite of this, he was out of a job. The Prohibition Unit had suspended him while it conducted its own investigation, and the inquiry that followed turned up various incidents of allegedly immoral and improper conduct by a government agent during the exercise of his duties. After these allegations emerged, he was fired.

However, he still managed to get himself deputized to carry out Prohibition raids (supported by Klan members) all over the region. Most of his raids were

The Shelton brothers. *Left to right*: Carl, Earl and Bernie. *Illinois State Historical Library*.

aimed at "foreigners and Catholics," and he began wreaking havoc with the appointed law enforcement officials in the towns and counties where he was operating. War loomed between the Klan and those who opposed it, and it erupted on February 8, 1924.

Young's actions had shaken the stability that bootleggers had created in the area. The arrangement that they had with the local law enforcement community had broken down because Young and the Klan conspicuously excluded local law officers from the planning and execution of their liquor raids.

The most powerful of the local bootleggers were the Shelton brothers, Carl, Earl and Bernie, farm boys from Wayne County who had established a profitable enterprise supplying alcohol to area saloons and roadhouses. When the Sheltons finally realized that their opponents couldn't be bought off or controlled, they began trying to protect their interests by recruiting gunmen into their ranks. In addition, local anti-Klan men formed a society called the Knights of the Flaming Circle, and while its members were fewer in number than those of the Klan, it included the Sheltons and anyone else who stood to suffer from the Klan's war on the liquor business. Another prominent member of the Knights, and likely the organizer, was Ora Thomas, a World War I veteran, bootlegger and bitter foe of the Klan. With dangerous men like Thomas and the Sheltons involved, a violent confrontation between the Knights and the Ku Klux Klan was inevitable.

One night, during one of Young's raids, a Shelton roadhouse was attacked. The raid was led by Young and Caesar Cagle, a Herrin constable who had once been a bootlegger himself. Earl Shelton was in the roadhouse when the raiders broke down the door and stormed inside. After the roadhouse was wrecked, Earl was placed against a wall and was ordered to list the names of the officials that the Sheltons were paying off. Shelton refused, and Cagle beat him with a pistol until he lay bleeding on the floor. Earl swore that he would remember the constable and, one day, would seek his revenge. That day turned out to be February 8, when Cagle was shot to death on the streets of Herrin, Illinois.

When word of Cagle's death reached Young, the Klan converged on Herrin. Hundreds of Klan members began patrolling the city streets, looking for Cagle's killers. Cars were stopped and their occupants questioned. Warrants were sworn out by Klansmen, and when it was learned that Ora Thomas was at the Herrin Hospital, having been injured in a violent clash earlier that night, the Klan tried to storm the building and demanded entrance from Dr. J.T. Black, the hospital administrator. When he refused, the Klan opened fire on the building, endangering the lives of doctors, nurses and innocent patients. Men inside the building returned the gunfire, and to the horror of the noncombatants of Herrin, the battle raged on for several hours. Only the arrival of state militia troops brought an end to the siege. A coroner's inquest cleared Ora Thomas of any role in Cagle's murder. Instead, it was determined that Carl and Earl Shelton had fired the fatal shots. The Sheltons had already fled from Herrin and reportedly headed south to Florida, where they could lay low for a while.

Meanwhile, the United States District Court in Danville began trying the cases of more than two hundred people accused of liquor violations as a result of Young's raids. The most prominent defendants were Ora Thomas and Charlie Birger, a bootlegger who was already on his way to becoming one of the most notorious figures in the history of Illinois crime. Deputy marshals were constantly on edge in the courthouse, watching for guns and waiting to see if violence was going to break out. One fistfight nearly occurred when Young cursed at Birger as the two men met in a courthouse corridor. Birger, as it turned out, received the heaviest sentence handed down by Judge Walter Lindley during these trials: one year in jail and several fines. Ora Thomas received a four-month sentence in addition to fines.

But Young had problems of his own. The special grand jury in Herrin presented its findings on March 14. It returned ninety-nine indictments, almost all of them involving men who took part in the attack on the hospital. The hardest hit was S. Glenn Young, who was charged with false imprisonment, kidnapping, assault with attempt to murder, malicious mischief, parading with arms and attempting to overthrow the civil authorities, along with other things. The jury singled Young out, stating that his "reign of terror," which began on February 8, came from "oppression and persecution by the so-called Ku Klux Klan." It contended that the attack on the hospital was "unlawful and without any justification whatever" and was a "most amazing display of mob violence." Young was nothing more than a power-mad renegade who, along with his cohorts, attempted to "overthrow the civil authorities in Herrin and Williamson County, seize and imprison the sheriff and the mayor, and take upon themselves the task of government without any legal authority."

Not surprisingly, the Klan reacted angrily to the grand jury findings. A protest parade was held on March 17, an event that showed that the Klan, despite Young's questionable tactics, still had strong support in the region. The parade included merchants; professional men, women and children; Protestant ministers; and, of course, Young bringing up the rear. When the parade ended, many of the participants went to the city hall and signed bonds for the men under indictment. The support for the Klan continued as its candidates managed to sweep the primary election in April. They celebrated with a procession through Marion and a cross burning.

This may have appeared to bode well for the Klan's strong-arm man, S. Glenn Young. Behind closed doors, though, Klan leaders in the county who had been paying Young well for his services were unhappy with his reckless behavior. Most were in favor of getting rid of him but knew that they had to move cautiously as they tried to cut ties with the still-popular figure. Fortunately for them, problems in East St. Louis provided a distraction.

During the early months of 1924, the Klan had been experiencing difficulties in East St. Louis, discord that became so bad that the local Klan's charter had been revoked. Illinois' grand dragon, Charles G. Palmer, turned to Young and asked him to investigate what was going on. Young readily agreed, seeing his assignment as an invitation to take over the organization in East St. Louis.

Meanwhile, the Shelton brothers had ended their stay in Florida and returned to Illinois. They were also headed for East St. Louis, which was their original base of operations. The Sheltons were aware that they were soon to face a jury trial on the Cagle murder charge, but they surrendered themselves to the authorities and filed $10,000 bonds to ensure their appearance in court. They were not only confident that they could beat the murder charge but also decided to end the Klan's stranglehold on their business by getting rid of S. Glenn Young.

On May 23, 1924, Young was at a rally in Herrin, where he boasted to the assembled crowd that he was leaving for East St. Louis to clean up the city. Among the people listening to Young as he shouted from the running board of his Lincoln sedan were the Shelton brothers. They watched as he climbed into his car and drove away, accompanied only by Maude, his young wife of three years. When Young left, the Sheltons joined two of their gunmen, Jack Skelcher and Charlie Briggs, and followed him in a Dodge touring car. They followed at a short distance, never pulling up close to Young's car until it reached a desolate, unpaved stretch of road that locals called the Okaw Bottoms.

Suddenly, the Dodge, with Bernie Shelton at the wheel, pulled up alongside Young's Lincoln, and the bootleggers opened fire on the Klansman and his wife. The cars locked bumpers for a moment and then broke loose, sending Young's car down an embankment. The door burst open; Young tumbled out and scurried for shelter under the automobile.

The Sheltons fired a few more shots in his direction and then sped away, leaving Young and his wife, both wounded, to be rescued by passing motorists. Both were transported to St. Elizabeth's Hospital in Belleville. Maude was taken in an ambulance, and Young was driven in his own car by one of the motorists who came upon the scene of the attack. Young, who had been shot in the leg, was not as badly hurt as his wife, whose eyesight was destroyed by a load of buckshot that hit her in the face.

The assassination attempt had been several days in the planning. A reward for killing Young had reached $1,800 in East St. Louis, where the arrival of Young to lead the local Klan was violently opposed. Although they had failed to kill Young, the Sheltons were hailed as heroes by gangsters and many politicians in East St. Louis, who didn't want a repeat of what happened in Herrin in their city. Many figured that the Sheltons deserved at least part of the bounty, and they were awarded $600.

Word of the attack soon reached Klan members, and they rallied behind Young, descending on St. Elizabeth's Hospital to establish an armed guard around the rooms of Young and his wife. Armed patrols surrounded the hospital, and Young himself kept two automatic pistols under his pillow.

Other Klansmen and their supporters went looking for revenge. The attempted murder sparked outrage among those still loyal to Young in Southern Illinois. On the same night as the attack, a large group of Klansmen in the Herrin area was appointed as deputies and, acting on a tip that Young's attackers were heading to the city, set up a series of roadblocks. On the morning of Saturday, May 25, a Dodge touring car that matched the description of the one used in the attack on Young tried to run a roadblock between Carterville and Herrin. Klansmen fired on the car, and it swerved and smashed into another vehicle on the road. Two men tried to run from the wreck but were shot down by the Klansmen. One of them, Jack Skelcher, was killed in the volley of fire. The other man, who was only slightly wounded, was Charlie Briggs. Four days later, several Klansmen were charged with Skelcher's murder.

Young pushed for indictments in his attack. He swore out warrants for attempted murder against Charlie Briggs and the Sheltons, whom he claimed to have seen in the Dodge with the other two men. Carl and Earl were likely there, but it's almost impossible that Young could have seen them. Regardless, the case would never go to trial, in spite of a preliminary hearing where Young showed up with thirty carloads of armed Klansmen to identify the assailants. Young named the Sheltons and Briggs as his attackers, and a justice of the peace bound the trio over to a November grand jury while releasing them on bond. Young was angry that the men were released, and neither he nor his wife showed up for the grand jury.

On August 30, 1924, the case against the Shelton brothers for the murder of Caesar Cagle came to trial. Before the jury could hear any of the evidence against them, Delos Duty, the state's attorney for Williamson County, moved that the case be dismissed. He had insufficient evidence against the Sheltons to prosecute, and his only witness, Tim Cagle, the father of the dead man and a justice of the peace in Carterville, stated that he had come to believe that the Sheltons had not murdered his son. Judge Bowen granted the motion of the state's attorney, and the Shelton brothers were freed.

A half hour after the Sheltons were released, Sheriff George Galligan went to the Herrin garage of John Smith, a local Klan leader, to seize an automobile that was behind held there—the Dodge car driven by Jack Skelcher on the day of his death and likely the same car used during the attack on Young. Galligan was accompanied by a number of anti-Klansmen, including Ora Thomas, special deputy J.H. "Bud" Allison and the Shelton brothers, Earl, Bernie and Carl. Galligan demanded the car, and when the attendant didn't move fast enough, one of the men hit him with a gun barrel. This resulted in a fistfight, which attracted attention outside on the street. One car that drove slowly past was filled with Klansmen, and it was halted by some of Galligan's men.

Suddenly, a shot rang out, and it was followed by more shots in the garage and out on the street. By the time the shootout ended, six men were dead, and several others, including Galligan and Carl and Earl Shelton, were wounded. Bud Allison, the special deputy, was one of the dead men. The other victims were three Klansmen, an innocent bystander and Chester Reid, who happened to be walking past the garage when the fighting broke out and tried to get everyone to put away their pistols. Aside from knowing just how many men were dead, it was impossible to tell what had really happened in the garage. The public accepted it as one more violent event in the ongoing war between the Ku Klux Klan and those who opposed it.

Another contingent of national guardsmen was dispatched to the area, quelling any additional threats of violence. Herrin had once again become a city under martial law, and even law-abiding citizens began carrying guns with them when they went out, never sure if they might end up in the middle of the next bloody mêlée.

That violent event occurred on January 24, 1925, when Young, who had been ousted from the Klan, and Ora Thomas had their final confrontation. On the street, Thomas bumped into Young and some of his hangers-on. By this time, only a fanatical few followers still clung to Young's coattails. They exchanged words, but Thomas pushed past and headed for home and the supper table. Later that night, Thomas narrowly missed being killed by stray gunfire. He walked down the street to the European Hotel and ran into Young, who was in the middle of an argument with a man in the cigar store.

Thomas walked inside, his hand on the butt of the pistol that he carried in his overcoat pocket. When he entered, an onlooker glanced toward Thomas and then quickly went out the back door. Alerted by the man's startled movement, Young swung around to look behind him. He backed toward the door, his eyes quickly taking in the hand that Thomas had in his overcoat pocket. He snapped, "Don't pull that gun, Ora."

In an instant, both men had drawn guns and began firing. The roaring sound of gunfire, accompanied by the sounds of men screaming and glass breaking, filled the room. Then there was silence. When the smoke cleared, those who dared enter the cigar store found four bodies on the floor. Two of Young's guards, Ed Forbes and Homer Warren, were dead. Young and Ora Thomas lay dying, their bullets having struck each other. Both men succumbed to their wounds in pools of blood on the floor of the store.

That night, no member of the Herrin police force dared to leave his home. Klansmen patrolled the city, stopping every car that attempted to enter. The first military troops arrived during the early morning hours, and their first act was to disarm the Klansmen and send them home. The town was as quiet as the grave.

Both Young and Thomas were buried in the days that followed, bringing only a temporary end to the violence.

THE SHELTON-BIRGER WAR

In 1926, a series of violent events mystified the people of Southern Illinois. One man's body was found in the middle of a dusty road north of Herrin, a bullet wound to his head. Another man was beaten in his automobile, unable or unwilling to identify his attackers. A few days later, a notorious character known as "Oklahoma Curly" was killed in a roadhouse on the outskirts of the city. Four days later, three gunmen held up an illegal gambling parlor in the basement of the European Hotel and made off with $3,000 and the watches, jewelry and pistols of the patrons. Then, a short time later, a young Herrin man was shot four times while taking part in a robbery at another local roadhouse.

The newspapers and local officials assumed these were random events and encouraged everyone to remain calm about this recent wave of violence.

However, the murders continued. On a Sunday night in late August, Harry Walker and an ex-convict named Smith shot each other to death in what appeared to be a personal disagreement. Many found it to be a bit ominous, though, when one of the Shelton brothers showed up at the coroner's inquest. Yet, in spite of the fact that Walker had been a Herrin policeman and the son of the former chief of police, another local paper shrugged off the incident as "a war between kindred tribes" and compared the violence to the bootlegger battles taking place in Chicago during the same time period. It urged people to just ignore the violence in the same way that people in the big cities did and let the gangsters kill one another off.

But the bloody events were getting hard to ignore. On the night of September 12, "Wild Bill" Holland, Mack Pulliam and Pulliam's wife left a roadhouse near Herrin. As they climbed into their automobile, two men came out of the shadows and attacked them. As the three victims lay bleeding and unconscious in the back of the car, the assailants drove the vehicle into Herrin and parked it in front of the hospital. When the occupants were discovered, Holland was dead, and Pulliam was in serious condition. Both of the men were friends of the late Harry Walker and acquaintances of the Sheltons.

Two days later, Pulliam's family, who were worried about his safety in Herrin, decided to move the injured man to a hospital in Benton. His mother rode in the ambulance with him and his wife, who had come away from the attack with only cuts and bruises, followed in another car. Just south of Benton, an automobile filled with armed men roared past the ambulance and then swung across the road to force it to stop. After lining everyone up at gunpoint, the gunmen forced their way into the ambulance. Pulliam's mother, terrified for her son's life, threw herself across his body and refused to move, even when prodded with gun barrels. Refusing to kill the woman just to get to her son, the gunmen beat Pulliam unconscious with their gun butts and drove away. Later, when he arrived at the hospital in Benton, Pulliam refused to talk about the incident, and no one in his party could, or would, identify the attackers.

It was becoming hard to ignore the fact that a gang war seemed to be in progress. After the Ku Klux Klan had abandoned the region, bootleggers and gamblers had started to openly operate again. Roadhouses sprang up overnight and soon outnumbered those that had existed prior to the raids by Young and the Klan. They quickly became a gathering place for criminals, and now it seemed the outlaws and gangsters were fighting amongst themselves. Why they were fighting—and who was fighting whom—was not yet clear.

The mystery was soon solved. One day in early October, people on the street in Marion noticed a large truck as it passed through town, heading east. They took notice of the truck because it was so unusual. In place of the standard bed, the truck was equipped with a steel tank that was filled with men who were heavily armed with rifles and Thompson submachine guns. They made no effort to conceal their weapons as they drove through town in what can best be described as a makeshift armored personnel carrier. The men in the truck found the people they were searching for near Harrisburg, where they came upon Art Newman and his wife driving westward on the highway. They opened fire on the car, and Mrs. Newman was wounded, but not seriously. Newman came through the volley of shots unscathed. Before the truck could be turned around, the Newmans sped away to safety.

Art Newman was a gambler, bootlegger and former associate of the Shelton brothers. He had recently broken ties with them and began working with rival gangster Charlie Birger, with whom he had been visiting in Harrisburg. Birger had been allied with the Sheltons during the battles with the Klan, but according to rumor, a falling out had occurred, and now the two factions were bitter enemies. Stories spread across the area, and many wondered if the attack on the Newmans confirmed the rumors of war between Birger and the Sheltons.

If the attempted murder of Art Newman was not confirmation enough, then the retaliatory attack on a Shelton roadhouse a few days later clenched things in the minds of most interested observers. The roadhouse had not been occupied for several weeks, but on this particular night, lights were seen inside. Several carloads of armed men pulled up outside and opened fire on the place. Moments later, they battered down the door; smashed the chairs, tables and glasses; and riddled the interior with bullets. Soon afterward, carrying their guns, they swaggered into the restaurant of the Jefferson Hotel and informed the staff that if anyone wanted to know who shot up the Shelton roadhouse, tell them "Charlie Birger did it."

Less than two weeks later, on the morning of October 26, the body of a Birger gunman called "High Pockets" McQuay was found lying along an old dirt road between Herrin and Johnston City. A bullet-marked Ford was angled off the road nearby. That same day, the body of Ward "Casey" Jones, another of Birger's men, was discovered in a creek near the town of Equality. Birger blamed the Sheltons for both murders and swore revenge.

By all signs, an all-out war was inevitable.

Charlie Birger was an unusual man. Those who met him for the first time were always impressed by his handsome appearance and his pleasant manner. His handshake was hearty, his smile was quick and the riding breeches and leather jacket that he customarily wore were always neat and

Bootlegger and gangster Charlie Birger would become a close ally with the Shelton brothers during their battles with the Ku Klux Klan. Later, for unknown reasons, the men would become bitter enemies. *Illinois State Historical Library*.

clean. Just under six feet tall, he carried himself with erect military bearing and looked younger than mid-forties, his actual age. He usually wore two guns in holsters and could often be seen sporting a well-oiled Thompson submachine gun.

Birger's dark skin and hair indicated his immigrant heritage. He was born to Russian immigrant parents in New York, and while still a child, his family moved to St. Louis. He was raised in the city and then in Glen Carbon, a coal town near East St. Louis. In 1901, he joined the Thirteenth U.S. Cavalry and served in the Spanish-American War. Afterward, he worked as a cowboy in South Dakota and then drifted back to East St. Louis. He became involved in saloons and gambling and, after Prohibition, became a bootlegger.

In East St. Louis, he would become friends with the men who would go on to become his deadly enemies just a few years later. These friends were the Shelton brothers—Carl, Earl and Bernie; together they would battle the powerful Ku Klux Klan.

The Sheltons were an integral part of the violence in the region. They grew up in Southern Illinois; their father had moved to Wayne County from Kentucky, married a local girl and started farming. The boys were brought up on the farm but from their early youth showed an aversion to hard work. As they got older, Carl and Earl began leaving home for months at a time to drive taxicabs in St. Louis and East St. Louis. When he was old enough, Bernie joined them. The boys sought out trouble, and all of them were soon mixed up with the law.

In the fall of 1915, Earl was convicted of armed robbery and sentenced to eighteen months at the Illinois State Penitentiary at Pontiac. About the same time, Carl was arrested in St. Louis and charged with petty larceny. He was sentenced to a year in a workhouse. Bernie was arrested in a stolen car while Earl was still in prison. He was also sentenced to a year in the workhouse but was paroled.

After Carl and Earl served out their sentences, both of them went to work in the Illinois coalmines, but around 1920, they moved back to East St. Louis, where Bernie was now living. They went into the bootlegging and gambling business and opened illegal joints in East St. Louis and the surrounding area. Their organization spread, and while the small towns in Southern Illinois each had their local toughs, gamblers and bootleggers, what they needed were the guns and brains to organize, something that was provided by the Shelton brothers. The Sheltons allowed the local boys to continue to operate, but only under their protection could they sell their liquor. Soon, the Sheltons were in command of a large portion of Southern Illinois.

During the Klan Wars, the Sheltons were regarded as some of the leaders of the anti-Klan faction, and Charlie Birger joined in with them to oppose the authority of S. Glenn Young. Once the Klan was defeated, the two rival operations began fighting each other, leading to more bloodshed and murder than Illinois had ever seen.

In the early 1920s, Charlie Birger moved to Harrisburg, and by this time, he was married to his second wife, had two children and was a successful "businessman." He had started a number of profitable speakeasies and brothels that offered not only liquor and prostitutes but gambling as well. Most of the establishments could be found in and around Harrisburg, including a notorious whoopee joint on West Poplar Street, but he also had others. The most famous of the time was the Halfway House, located between Marion and Johnston City.

Many chose to see Birger as a public benefactor rather than as a killer and bootlegger. In Harrisburg, he helped many people in need. One severe winter, he canvassed the town and sent coal to all of the poor families he could find. On another occasion, he purchased schoolbooks for children whose families could not afford to buy them. He let it be known that he would not permit Harrisburg residents to patronize his gambling tables because "you can't win in a professional game." He also claimed that he had prevented several robberies in town, and after the outbreak of gang violence, he took on the role of public protector.

In December 1923, Birger got caught up in one of the early bootlegging raids organized by S. Glenn Young and his Klan supporters. He spent time in jail and, after he got out, joined forces with the Sheltons. Birger had first met Carl Shelton in the fall of 1923 when he was in the Herrin Hospital recovering from wounds that he had received in the gunfight with Doering. The two men became personal friends and business associates in bootlegging and the slot-machine racket. The Sheltons were running bootleg liquor from the south for distribution in Southern Illinois and in the East St. Louis area. Birger allowed them to use Harrisburg as a layover and shipping point. During the Klan fighting, they stood together against Young's faction.

In 1924, Birger began building what would become his most prominent establishment, Shady Rest. Located about halfway between Marion and Harrisburg on Route 13, the roadhouse drew disreputable characters and customers from all over the region. It would become the base of Birger's illegal operations. Shady Rest opened for business later that year and offered bootleg liquor, gambling, cockfights and dog fights. During the day, business was light, so the place was often used as a layover by liquor runners traveling from Florida. They could then make the last leg of their trip into St. Louis after dark. Although notorious all over Southern Illinois, no police officials ever raided or bothered the place. It was no secret what it was being used for or that it had been built to withstand a siege if necessary. The building had been constructed with foot-thick log walls and a deep basement. Rifles, submachine guns and boxes of ammunition lined the walls, alongside canned food and water. Floodlights, supplied with electricity that was generated on the grounds, prevented anyone from sneaking up on Shady Rest in the night.

The place was very popular with the locals until the relationship between Birger and the Sheltons fell apart. After that, the bloody climate of the location kept many customers away.

Why the bloody rift developed between Birger and the Sheltons is unclear. Most likely, it was simply business that became personal. The two groups had originally united to fight against Young and the Klan's encroachment on their business. Once the Klan was wiped out, there was no one left to fight but each other. Others maintained that the real break between Birger and his former partners came as a result of his determination to protect the people of Harrisburg. According to his story, "Blackie" Armes and several of the Sheltons' gunmen (none of the brothers was in the group) robbed a Harrisburg businessman of a valuable diamond ring that they intended to hold until he redeemed it for cash. Birger was incensed over the robbery and forced them to return it. This led to resentment on the part of the Sheltons, sentiment that eventually led to violence.

But regardless of why the war started, it plunged all of Southern Illinois into chaos.

On the day before the bodies of Birger's men "High Pockets" McQuay and "Casey" Jones were found, Birger and several of his men called on Joe Adams, a slow, overweight man who worked as a roadhouse operator, a Stutz motor car dealer and as mayor of West City, a small town on the edge of Benton. Birger heard that the Sheltons had left their steel-tank truck, used in the attack on Art Newman, at Adams's garage for repairs. Birger demanded that Adams give it to him and in fact warned him that if he did not, he would "drill you so full holes people won't know your corpse."

Adams refused, and an argument ensued. Before he left, he told Adams to deliver the truck to Shady Rest. If he did so, he could save himself "a lot of trouble with undertakers and caskets, if you know what I mean."

Instead of complying, Adams called on the county authorities for protection. They refused, so he asked the Sheltons for help. They sent a number of armed men to Adams's garage and waited for Birger to return. When the state's attorney learned of their presence, he ordered them to leave the county. But they did not leave quietly.

Early the next morning, a farmer who lived next to a Birger roadhouse near Johnston City saw fifteen or twenty men sneak out of the nearby woods and open fire on the place. In a few minutes, it caught on fire. The men laughed and shouted as they watched the flames, and while passing motorists slowed down as they saw the fire, none dared to stop. As the sun was rising, the men slipped back into the woods, climbed into their cars and drove away.

On a Saturday night in early November 1926, a Birger associate named John Milroy was machine-gunned as he left a roadhouse in the town of Colp. The mayor and the chief of police, called from another roadhouse nearby, were shot at from the darkness as they got out of their car. The mayor was fatally wounded, but the police chief, who ran at the sound of the first shot, escaped with a shattered hand. Both men, it was said, were enemies of the Sheltons.

A few days later, a homemade bomb was tossed from a speeding car toward Shady Rest. The bomb had been intended for the building, but it missed, and Birger's hideout was unharmed. Two days later, machine-gunners (allegedly sent by Birger) shot up the home of Joe Adams, the mayor of West City.

Then, hours later, the only bombs ever dropped during aerial warfare in America fell on Shady Rest. In full daylight, an airplane flew low over Birger's hideout as his men watched. Three bundles were thrown from the cockpit. They turned out to be dynamite bound around bottles of nitroglycerine. One fell apart in the air, but two fell to the ground near the barbecue stand. The "bombs" were so poorly constructed that they never exploded. The attack was attributed to the Sheltons, repaying Birger for shooting up Joe Adams's home.

The following week, a more effective bomb was thrown in response, this time by the Birger gang. It exploded in front of Joe Adams's house, damaging the front porch, blowing the door off its hinges and shattering the windows. Had the bomb landed just ten feet closer to the house, everyone in the house, including Adams, his wife and his brother, would have been killed. As it was, no one was injured—but it wouldn't stay that way for long.

On Sunday afternoon, December 12, two men came to the door of Adams's house and told his wife they had a letter from Carl Shelton. When he answered his wife's call, one of the men handed Adams a note. While he read it, both men pulled guns from their coats and shot him in the stomach and chest. He lived just long enough to tell his wife that he hadn't recognized the killers.

The next day, at the coroner's inquest, Mrs. Adams blamed the killing on Charlie Birger. During the last several weeks, he had telephoned frequently, sometimes as often as three times a day. Once, he had asked her if she had much life insurance on her husband. When she said that she didn't, Birger replied, "Well, you'd better get a lot more because we're going to kill him, and you'll need it."

The gang war soon reached its climax. Just after midnight on January 9, 1927, a farmer who lived a short distance from Shady Rest was awakened by five or six gunshots that seemed to come from the vicinity of the roadhouse. He went back to sleep and, a few moments later, was shocked awake by a massive explosion. Rushing to his window, he saw that Shady Rest had been blown apart. A few seconds later, another explosion rocked the structure; it was so strong that he felt his own house tremble on its foundation. The fire at Shady Rest burned so hot that no one dared approach the ruins until morning. By then, it was merely ashes and burned embers. However, among the remains were four bodies, charred beyond recognition.

Everyone said that the war was now over. The destruction of Shady Rest was sure to make Charlie Birger realize that he was finished and that if he attempted to continue the hostilities he would lose his life, just as he had lost his headquarters. That's what everyone thought and what observers predicted would mark the end of the war—but they were wrong.

From all appearances, Charlie Birger was finished. Shady Rest had been destroyed, his men were scattered and his rivals had taken over his bootlegging business. No matter how bad things looked, though, he believed that he would still manage to beat the Sheltons in the end. He failed to best them with machine guns and dynamite, but he dealt a blow against them by using the might of the U.S. government.

Almost two years earlier, in January 1925, a post office messenger in Collinsville had been robbed of a mine payroll adding up to about $21,000. The crime had remained unsolved. Birger contacted the postal inspector and managed to convince him that the Sheltons had pulled the job. In November 1926, a federal grand jury returned secret indictments against the three Shelton brothers and, one by one, they were arrested and released on bond. Birger and some of his cronies testified at the trial, and the three Shelton brothers were sentenced to twenty-five years in the federal penitentiary.

Charlie Birger had technically won the gang war for Southern Illinois and had put his rivals out of business in the region, but he soon realized that his victory would not last. On April 29, he had been picked up and charged at the Franklin County Jail in Benton for the murder of Joe Adams. Birger denied that he had anything to do with the killing of Adams, but he was also blamed for the deaths of the men who were killed when Shady Rest burned down and for the death of Lory Price, a highway patrolman and friend, and his wife, Ethel, who had been kidnapped and killed. After a lengthy trial, Birger was found guilty of murder and hanged on April 9, 1928.

THE SHELTONS MOVE TO PEORIA

Unfortunately, Charlie Birger was still alive to see his plans to destroy the Shelton brothers fall apart. Edmund Burke, one of the attorneys for the Shelton brothers, filed a motion in the United States court in Springfield asking that they be granted a new trial. To support the motion, he produced an affidavit from Harry Dungey, one of the prosecution's chief witnesses.

In it, Dungey swore that he had perjured himself when he testified that he had seen Carl and Bernie Shelton near Collinsville on the day of the mail robbery. Birger, he claimed, had threatened to kill him unless he testified as he did. The affidavit did the trick, and the Sheltons were granted a new trial and released on bond.

The Sheltons never served time for the mail robbery that Birger managed to get them convicted for. They continued to use East St. Louis as their headquarters for gambling, liquor and prostitution. They remained there until an honest sheriff drove them out, unfortunately making room for mob organizers to turn the city into a major gambling spot.

The Sheltons then moved north to Peoria, which they found to be much more hospitable. During the late 1930s, they established themselves and began an operation that comprised most of the illegal rackets in downstate Illinois.

In those days, Peoria was a city that welcomed vice with open arms. One writer noted that it was the "sleaziest, the orneriest, the rottenest and rip-snortingest town this side of…well, this side of Chicago and that side of St. Louis. Its sins are legend." It was a place that officered a safe haven for gamblers and prostitutes, and a good number of the residents took advantage of the city's tolerance for gambling dens and brothels. When Carl Shelton established the brothers' operations there, illegal wagering was welcomed with open arms, especially by politicians and cops, who saw it as a great way to make a little extra money. Not surprisingly, the Sheltons soon became immune to prosecution.

Carl Shelton might never have achieved the notoriety that he did in Peoria if other outside gangsters had not already bungled their moves to take over operations in the area. There were several botched kidnap attempts on local gambling operators that terrified not only the would-be victims but the politicians that protected them as well. One failed attempt occurred in 1930. The victim was Clyde Garrison, the operator of the Windsor Club on Fulton Street, one of the biggest gaming houses in the Midwest. His wife was killed during the attempt, and he needed no convincing that bringing in the Sheltons to protect the still locally controlled gambling interests was the right thing to do.

Prior to the 1940s, Shelton worked for Garrison, protecting his interests and those of other local gamblers from outsiders but not upstaging Garrison's role as the head of Peoria operations. The alliance between them was lucrative for both sides, but things started to sour amid the gambling upswing in the area at the start of World War II. No one knows what caused the falling out (just like in the war with Charlie Birger), but most believe that

Carl Shelton, the leader of the gang. By the time the brothers relocated to Peoria, Carl was considered the best-known gangster in Illinois, outside of Chicago. *Bowen Archives at Southern Illinois University–Edwardsville.*

Carl Shelton began taking a role in the political side of things, which had always been Garrison's side of the deal. Garrison resisted Shelton's efforts for a time, but not for long. Realizing that he lacked the muscle to take on the Sheltons, Garrison got out of gambling and went into the wholesale liquor business.

After that, Carl had the field to himself, and from 1941 to 1945, the Sheltons' operations prospered like never before. Thanks to the dangerous reputation that the Sheltons enjoyed, they managed to maintain order among the unsavory elements in Peoria in the early 1940s. This was much to the delight of the city's political leaders, especially Mayor Edward Nelson Woodruff, who was perhaps the most corrupt Illinois mayor behind "Big Bill" Thompson, Al Capone's man in Chicago.

Carl established a business network that combined his aboveboard activities with the illicit ones. The network required the enlistment of a number of different individuals to oversee things. For example, the Shelton Amusement Co., which was a legitimate operation, was run by Shelton's trusted man, Jack Ashby. The amusement company handled jukeboxes and other legal coin-operated devices, while also delivering slot machines to the back rooms of bars and taverns throughout the area.

The Sheltons' hold on Peoria ended after the 1945 elections. A new mayor, Carl O. Triebel, came into office and became known as a reformer, even though he never ran on that platform. However, he did decide to start cracking down on gambling, prostitution and anything else that stained the reputation of the city. Just before he took office, Triebel held a meeting with Carl Shelton and informed him of his plans. When Shelton realized that Triebel meant business, he shrugged and simply said, "Well, I guess that'll give me more time to farm."

Triebel, who also owned farmland, sat with Shelton for almost thirty minutes, talking about agriculture. Then they shook hands, and Carl left his office, never to see the new mayor again. By this time in his life, Carl really did want to retire to his farming and oil interests in Wayne County.

In the city of Peoria, pressure from Triebel forced gambling underground, but this was not the case in Peoria County. Carl Shelton may have abandoned his interests in the area, but Bernie served notice that he planned to take over

Bernie Shelton, the youngest and most dangerous of the Shelton brothers, was a heavy drinker and known for partying and carrying on with a string of women. He was shot to death outside of the Parkway Tavern in Peoria, his headquarters in the city. *Bowen Archives at Southern Illinois University–Edwardsville.*

what his brother left behind. The changeover was easily handled for Bernie because the rough brawler with the terrible temper struck fear in the hearts of friends and foes alike. He secured a free hand for the rackets through financial arrangements with certain county officials and moved the Shelton headquarters from downtown Peoria to the Parkway Tavern, an unimposing bar on Farmington Road, just outside the city limits.

With Bernie now in command, some assumed that Carl was out of the Shelton Gang. Others were not so sure because he still lived part time in Peoria and met with Bernie on many occasions at the Parkway Tavern. He was, at the very least, an advisor to the vice network that he had created. In addition, south of Peoria, Carl—not Bernie—remained in charge of the numerous gambling operations, large and small, that were scattered throughout rural parts of central Illinois. Regardless, with Carl stepping back from his highly visible role in Peoria, other gangsters began eyeing the Sheltons' territory. After years of a hands-off policy toward the Sheltons, the Chicago Outfit finally decided to curb the independence that had been given to them. The Outfit instructed its St. Louis emissaries to offer the Sheltons a deal that would bring them peacefully into the syndicate. If that didn't work, the Outfit certainly had other methods at its disposal—methods that became necessary when the Sheltons refused to deal.

Following World War II, the Outfit, with connections to the national syndicate created by Meyer Lansky and Charles "Lucky" Luciano in New York, had expanded its underworld dealings across the country. After taking over operations in St. Louis, the Outfit inherited the services of a number of gangsters who had formerly worked with the Sheltons. Two of the most prominent were "Blackie" Armes and Frank "Buster" Wortman.

The defection of Armes and Wortman occurred in the early 1940s after the end of their prison incarceration for assaulting federal agents during a raid on a still in Collinsville in 1933. When the two were inmates at Alcatraz, the Outfit managed to make things more bearable for them on the inside, earning their loyalty. In addition, when the two were released from prison, they claimed that Carl Shelton did nothing for them. Wortman soon went on to build an empire for himself in southwestern Illinois, but Armes was gunned down in a nightclub in Herrin in late 1944.

Word soon circulated that either Carl or Bernie was worth $10,000 to anyone who brought either man to Chicago alive. But no one could get close to the Sheltons, who refused all contact with both St. Louis and Chicago gangsters. Soon, the reward was changed. It was still $10,000, but it was now for either of the Sheltons—dead or alive. Spurred by the reward, a gang of Chicago gunmen set a trap to ambush Carl and Bernie at the Parkway Tavern. Carl got wind of the plans, though, and several carloads of Shelton gunmen showed up at the bar instead of the brothers.

The Outfit gunmen soon returned to Chicago, but they, or someone else with murderous intentions toward the Sheltons, would be back. In 1946, a number of Shelton associates were slaughtered. Frank Kraemer, a slot machine operator and tavern owner, was shot to death by an unknown gunman in February. Seven months later, the body of Joel Nyberg, who worked as muscle for the Sheltons, was found shot to death on a local golf course. A month after that, Phillip Stumpf, another slot machine operator, was gunned down while driving home from a bar on Big Hollow Road. With each murder, the level of protection afforded the Sheltons grew smaller, and when the killing went unanswered, many came to believe that the Sheltons were unable to defend their friends. More defections followed, but the Sheltons continued their operations, defying the St. Louis and Chicago gangsters.

As gambling became even more widespread in Illinois after the election of sympathetic governor Dwight Green, Outfit racketeers became increasingly frustrated over the continued presence of the Sheltons in Northern Illinois. When the Sheltons refused to give in to Chicago and St. Louis demands, the murders of a number of their associates followed, but to little effect. Nothing, it seemed, could eliminate the Sheltons' influence as long as Carl was alive. Attempts to kill him in Peoria or to take him out somewhere else failed, but his enemies knew that his luck couldn't hold out forever.

After Carl began spending more time in Wayne County, it seemed at first that the odds of eliminating him had grown longer. But all was not well for Shelton at home. His farm prospered, and his Basin Oil Well Service Company in Fairfield was doing well. He seemed to be on his way to becoming a successful, legitimate businessman, and many in the area accorded him great respect. His only problems seemed to come from some of his neighbors in the Pond Creek area. One squabble followed another, mostly between Carl and members of the Harris-Vaughn clan, led by "Black Charlie" Harris, a former Shelton associate. Like Wortman and Armes, Harris served time in Leavenworth, and when he got out, he came to believe that the Sheltons owed him more than just their continued friendship and a little business every once in a while. He also became convinced that Carl had swindled him out of some Wayne County farmland, a belief that enhanced his hatred for the Sheltons. Harris became the protector of anyone on the outs with Carl and Earl, who also lived in Fairfield. The whole thing might have been dismissed as nothing more than a local feud if not for the presence of Harris, who was a killer and well acquainted with the territory and habits of the Sheltons.

The assassination of Carl Shelton was foreshadowed by two events that occurred in 1947. Either of the events, or perhaps both of them, may have led to Carl's death, although we will never know for sure since his murder remains unsolved.

The first event was the murder of Ray Doughtery, a former Shelton gunman who had aligned himself with Roy Armes, the brother of the murdered "Blackie" Armes, who had become a lieutenant of Frank Wortman. Doughtery's body was found blasted full of holes on the shore of Crab Orchard Lake, near Carbondale. The local coroner linked the unsolved murder to "trouble between gangs," but many suspected that the killing was the first step in a planned resurgence by the Sheltons. Rumors were running wild that the Sheltons were strengthening their hold in rural parts of Illinois and contemplating a comeback in the East St. Louis area. If true, then the murder of Ray Doughtery was seen as a warning sign of the Sheltons' intent. To the syndicate, this meant that Carl Shelton had to be taken out if new gang warfare was to be avoided.

The second event, brought on by Carl Shelton himself, involved the beating of Charlie Harris's nephew. This was an ongoing part of the Pond Creek feud and resulted from the theft of some of the Sheltons' blooded Black Angus cattle. In searching for the culprits, an angry Carl Shelton caught up with the young man and beat him badly. Then, later that same day, Harris's nephew was shot and seriously wounded by unknown assailants outside Fairfield. Harris was outraged by these events.

On the morning of October 23, 1947, Carl went out to the farm to take care of some things. He drove up Pond Creek Road in a military surplus Jeep with two of his men following behind in a truck. When the vehicles reached a small bridge that had to be crossed to get to Carl's property, a volley of gunfire exploded from the surrounding woods. Carl toppled out of the Jeep and hit the ground. The other men scrambled out of the truck and scurried for cover in a ditch. The two men survived, but Carl Shelton was dead—shot twenty-five times.

Two hours passed before the men could notify police and return to the scene of the attack. They were accompanied by the Wayne County sheriff, Hal Bradshaw, Lieutenant Ben Blades of the Illinois State Police and Earl Shelton. Carl's body was found in a ditch by the bridge on the east side of the road. His feet were about a foot from the top of the ditch, and his head and face were down in the bottom. The lawmen suggested that the body be left in that position until photographs could be taken, but Earl protested, saying that he didn't want his brother left lying like that.

When the body was moved, a gun was discovered underneath it. Earl identified it as Carl's revolver. Opening the weapon, Lieutenant Blades saw that five of the six shells had been fired. The officers searched the ground and found numerous empty cartridges and shells, many of which were a government type that was used in machine guns. Whoever the killers had been, whether Outfit gunmen or relatives of Charlie Harris, they had wanted to make sure that Carl Shelton was dead.

While new gang warfare seemed inevitable after Carl's murder, no trouble materialized during the funeral, which was the largest event that Fairfield had ever seen. The numerous law officers who were present ended up doing little more than directing traffic. It was hard to ignore the fact that the Sheltons and their men were wearing guns under their suit coats, but Earl did everything he could to ease the tension that gripped the area. He stated publicly that his family's only reaction to the murder would be for law enforcement to "take its usual course." Many found this hard to believe, especially since the general consensus was that Charlie Harris was somehow involved in the assassination. Harris was later arrested for the murder (he fled for a time because he claimed to fear reprisal from the Sheltons), but a grand jury was unable to indict him for the crime. Many reporters believed that Harris was not involved. Their theory was that the crime had been carried out by gunmen connected to the Chicago Outfit or by its allies in St. Louis. True to gangland tradition, the identities of the actual shooters remained a mystery.

There were many who suspected that the death of Carl Shelton would mean the end of the brothers' operations. As it turned out, however, the immediate reaction to Carl's death was mild by underworld standards. In the weeks that followed the murder, some Shelton associates closed down their gambling houses. Others handed over control of their operations to the Outfit, which was ecstatic about the demise of Carl Shelton. "Buster" Wortman, a man who may not have been an innocent bystander to Carl's murder, began to expand beyond the St. Clair and Madison County areas now that Carl Shelton was out of the way.

One part of the Shelton operations not affected by Carl's death was in Peoria, where Bernie was still running the family's gaming enterprises in the same way that he had been. He made it widely know that he was in firm control of the area and actually planned to expand the operation farther south into other parts of Illinois. Needless to say, this caused a ripple of unrest among the Chicago and St. Louis gangsters, who had taken it for granted that the Sheltons would crumble after the death of Carl. They approached Bernie with offers of peace, but he rebuffed their advances. The Outfit's response was predictable. Bernie had been a marked man before Carl's death, and the reward that had been offered for his life was still very much available. The Outfit wanted someone to collect it.

Throughout the early months of 1948, Bernie showed no signs of backing down. He continued his operations, kept up his payoffs to those who offered political protection and made sure that he stayed visible to those who might have some idea of moving in on his business. However, it was a tavern brawl that almost tripped him up. Bar fights were old, bad habits of his. He was lucky to have escaped prison time in the late 1930s after beating and shooting a man named Frank Zimmerman during a fight in a Cahokia bar. The fight at the Parkway Tavern on Memorial Day 1948 would turn out to be much more serious.

The fight reportedly started when Richard Murphy, a navy veteran from Peoria, began mouthing off about the ejection of a drunken patron from the bar. A fistfight started in the parking lot, resulting in Murphy being pummeled by Bernie and a couple of his men. One account from witnesses claimed that they pistol-whipped the man. During the fight, A.L. Hunt, the proprietor of a popular drive-in located across Farmington Road from the tavern, came over to try and break things up. Hunt, who was no friend of Shelton's, claimed that Bernie shoved a pistol into his back and marched him back across the road with dire warnings about minding his own business. As a result of the brawl, a Peoria County grand jury returned indictments against Bernie and the other two men for assault with intent to kill—a felony.

The bar fight might have been dismissed by most as a minor altercation, but not by the man who led the grand jury investigation, Roy P. Hull, the state's attorney for Peoria County. In the Illinois primary elections of that year, Hull was defeated in his bid for nomination for reelection to his post in the upcoming November election. One of those who helped to oppose Hull was Bernie Shelton, opposition that did not sit well with Hull. As a result, the indictment would plague Shelton for the rest of his life.

As it turned out, though, Bernie's life wouldn't last much longer. The first attempt on his life was to have occurred while he was on his way to Muscatine, Iowa, to sell some horses. Two cars filled with gunmen had waited for him along a highway near Galesburg, but Bernie never showed. By chance, he took another route to Muscatine and thwarted the plan.

The next attempt to kill him was planned for July 26. Bernie left his home at 10:00 a.m. on that hot Monday morning and drove to the Parkway Tavern to meet with a bartender named Alex Ronitis. Shelton wanted the bartender to follow him to a Peoria auto agency, where he planned to leave his car for some work. Ronitis would then return Shelton to the tavern.

Shelton spent about forty-five minutes handling some paperwork in his private office, and then he and Ronitis started to walk out together. However, Ronitis stepped back into the bar to get a pack of cigarettes, leaving Shelton to walk alone to his sedan in the parking lot. Bernie was unaware that, as he approached the car, he was in clear view of a man who was hiding in the brush at the bottom of a wooded hill behind the parkway. The man had a .351-caliber Winchester automatic rifle in his hands, and he fired a single shot. The bullet slammed into Bernie's chest, and he fell forward, slumped against his car. Witnesses later stated that they saw a well-dressed man run from the brush and jump into a green Chevrolet, which drove quickly away.

Ronitis was about to open the tavern door and come outside when he heard the rifle shot. After hesitating for a few seconds, he opened the door and saw Bernie kneeling next to his car. Ronitis started to move toward him, but Shelton waved him back. He held the door open as Bernie stumbled across the parking lot and into the tavern. Bernie heaved himself onto a barstool and told Ronitis and another bartender, Edward Connor, "I've been shot from the woods." He was bleeding badly from a chest wound.

Connor called for an ambulance, and when it arrived, Bernie insisted on walking to it. He collapsed on a stretcher inside and was driven to St. Francis Hospital. When he arrived in the emergency room, he asked an attendant to remove his shoes and his trousers, predicting that he was going to die. And he did, just a few minutes later.

As with the killing of Carl Shelton, Bernie's murder was never solved.

The death of Bernie Shelton brought an end to the era of the gang in Peoria. It also led to the end of the Shelton Gang itself, or what was left of it, in Illinois. Talk was heard about some of the Sheltons' most trusted men continuing the operations, but it never amounted to anything. Tragically, Bernie was not the last of the brothers to die. Roy, the eldest, was killed in June 1950, while driving a tractor on Earl's farm. Although he had a criminal record, he had never been associated with Carl, Earl and Bernie.

After Bernie's death, Earl, the last of the feared Shelton boys, was reluctant to venture too far away from Fairfield. As it turned out, though, trouble came looking for him.

On the night of May 24, 1949, Earl was wounded by one of three bullets fired through a window of the Sheltons' Farmers Club, located on the courthouse square in Fairfield. The window at the rear of the second-floor

Bernie Shelton's car was photographed outside of the Parkway Tavern on the day he was shot. A single bullet struck him as he walked out of the tavern's office toward his automobile. *Bowen Archives at Southern Illinois University–Edwardsville.*

gambling den was the only one in the establishment not painted black. To see into the interior of the club, the unknown gunman had climbed a ladder to the roof of a car dealership next to the club. From there, he had a clear view of Earl's back as he sat playing cards. Earl had laid down his cards and was talking to some friends when three shots shattered the window. One of the bullets struck him in the back. The gunman hurried down the ladder and disappeared.

Earl was rushed to Deaconess Hospital in Evansville, Indiana, but even though he had lost a lot of blood, he was not in danger of dying. An operation failed to find the bullet, but Earl recovered while those in Wayne County prepared for more violence.

The next attack against the remaining Sheltons occurred during the early morning hours of September 9, 1949. Residents along Elm Street were startled awake by the roar of gunfire coming from the home of "Little Earl" Shelton, a nephew who had been serving as a bodyguard for his uncle Earl. Little Earl was just arriving home in his Buick when the shots rang out. Although hit, he threw himself on the floor of his car, an act that probably saved his life. As his attackers sped away, he managed to draw his gun from a shoulder holster and fire several shots in their direction. He would later claim that the fleeing sedan had belonged to Charlie Harris. Once again,

Harris was charged with the crime, but the charges were later dismissed due to lack of evidence.

Once the attackers had fled, Little Earl managed to crawl out of his car, where his wife, Eleanor, found his bloody body next to the curb. She rushed him to the hospital in Evansville, and doctors found that he had been hit eight times, mostly in the lower parts of his body. The Fairfield police said that Earl's car had been struck twenty-one times, likely by machine gun fire. Miraculously, Earl survived the assault. He had served with valor in an army armored division during World War II and had been wounded in the invasion of Sicily. However, those wounds didn't compare to the ones that he suffered on the streets of his hometown.

The year 1950 became a time of open season on the Sheltons. Roy was killed and Earl was hit in the right arm but not seriously wounded when he and Little Earl were driving in the Pond Creek area, inspecting some oil drilling operations. Two weeks later, Little Earl was grazed when a shotgun and a rifle opened up on him in front of a garage a few miles west of Fairfield. He and a friend, Dellos Wylie, managed to make it out of the car and into the garage. The gunmen, hidden in some brush across the road, continued to fire at them. Wylie tried to escape from the building and was cut down with several bullets in his back, leaving him badly wounded.

After Roy's funeral, Sheriff Bradshaw, along with others in the community, suggested that the remaining Sheltons consider leaving the area. But Big Earl and Little Earl refused to consider the idea, vowing not to be driven out. Their resolve was weakened a short time later when a homemade bomb wrecked Earl's home. He and his wife, Earline, were lucky to survive the attack. The Sheltons were in bed when someone tossed a can filled with nitroglycerine through their front window. They were awakened by the sound of breaking glass, and while Earline telephoned the sheriff, Earl went out into the front room. Moments later, there was a deafening blast, and Earl was thrown back into the bedroom. The resulting fire swept through the house, and the Sheltons barely managed to make it to safety.

The loss of his home was enough to convince Earl that it was time to leave. A month and a half later, in January 1951, he and Earline, along with Little Earl and his family, left Illinois for good. They moved to Florida and settled in the Jacksonville area, which had been a favorite spot of the Sheltons during their bootlegging days.

Another notorious chapter in Illinois' criminal history had come to an end.

Two Heads in a Concrete Block

Traditionally, a lamp that is left burning in a window signifies a welcoming beacon for a loved one who is away. But that was not the explanation for the lamp that burned in the window of Warren Lincoln's home in Aurora in 1923.

Lincoln's young housekeeper, Marie Klein, explained the lamp to neighbors:

> *Mr. Lincoln is afraid—that's why he keeps the lamp lighted. He says someone is spying on him. He thinks Mrs. Lincoln and her brother have hired a person to "get" him. The light is a signal that has been fixed up between Mr. Lincoln and his brother. As long as it shines, it means everything is all right. If it goes out, Mr. Edward Lincoln is to grab his gun and run over there.*

Warren Lincoln, the neighbors all agreed, had good reasons for his fears. It was commonly known that there had been trouble in the family—but no one had any idea just how far that trouble would go.

At the time that Warren Lincoln began to fear for his life, he was a small, baldheaded, middle-aged former lawyer from Chicago who operated a greenhouse and nursery on the outskirts of Aurora. He lived on the property and operated the place in partnership with his brother, Edward, who lived about three hundred yards away. Poor health had caused Lincoln to retire from his law practice and leave Chicago. He moved to Aurora with his wife, the former Lina Shoup, and John, his teenage son from his first marriage. They arrived in the spring of 1920, and almost immediately, neighborhood tongues began to wag.

The Warren Lincoln home, where the drama between Lincoln and his wife and brother-in-law, Lina and Byron Shoup, played out. *Beacon News Archives*.

It was soon obvious that Mrs. Lincoln and her stepson did not get along. Frequent arguments and outright hostility caused the young man to move his bedroom out of the house and into the greenhouse. Later, he packed up and moved back to Chicago. He was heard to remark that the less he saw of Lina, the better.

The neighbors also knew that Mrs. Lincoln's large and unfriendly brother, Byron, was another source of unpleasantness in the household. Byron Shoup lived in Wichita, Kansas, and had first visited the Lincolns in early 1921. He had stayed until the middle of May. Later visits, which were always just as prolonged, had generated frequent quarrels in which Warren Lincoln inevitably got the worst of the argument, often resulting in bruises, cuts and black eyes.

The same neighbors who whispered about and watched the Lincoln home had seen Byron Shoup around the house during the first week or so of January 1923, but by the middle of the month, both he and Lina had disappeared. Warren Lincoln kept his thoughts about this development to himself, but his brother, Edward, was quick to report that Lina had run off with another man. Her brother, he said, had gone back to Kansas.

After a couple of weeks of Lina's absence, Warren filed for divorce. At the same time, the former attorney filed suit against Byron Shoup in the amount of $25,000 in damages, alleging that Byron had come between him and Lina and caused her to abandon their marriage.

John Lincoln came back from Chicago after his stepmother left and began working in the greenhouse with his father, uncle and two hired men. Two or three times each week, Marie Klein, the twelve-year-old daughter of a neighbor, came in to take care of the cleaning and the rest of the housework. Everything around the Lincoln home, for a change, seemed quiet and peaceful—but it was not meant to last.

That spring, John Lincoln got a new job and moved back to Chicago. About the same time, Warren Lincoln began putting the lamp in the window that faced his brother's house. He also made his first call to Aurora's chief of police, Frank Michels, and told him about a mysterious stranger who seemed to be spying on him and possibly intended him harm.

Lincoln claimed that he had tried to talk to the man several times, but every time he approached him, the stranger hurried away. He told Chief Michels that he was convinced the man was sent by Byron and Lina, who had likely heard about the suits he had filed against them. He also stated that he believed the stranger had been inside his house, possibly with others. Marie Klein had found a woman's handkerchief and some hairpins under the dining room table one day. Warren said that he was sure that the stranger had placed them there, possibly trying to frame him for his wife's disappearance.

He told the police chief that he had not heard from Lina in some time and didn't care if he ever did. Warren went on to describe how he believed she and her brother had tried to kill him on several occasions. One night, he had become sick after dinner, and he was sure the pair had tried to poison him. Two times, they had insisted so forcefully that he sample one of the dishes on the table that he refused to touch it. Another time, Lina made him a cup of cocoa, although she knew that Warren never drank the stuff. When he reminded her of that fact, Byron jumped out of his chair and told the smaller man that he would make him drink it if he had to. Instead, Warren poured it on the floor. Byron was so angry that he beat Warren, threw him into a closet and kept him locked up there for several hours. On another occasion, Byron brought him a cup of coffee. As he had never shown his brother-in-law such kind attention before, Warren got suspicious and exchanged his cup for Byron's when the other man wasn't looking. Byron became violently ill after drinking it.

When told that he should have reported these incidents to the authorities, Warren shook his head. "I don't like the idea of a public scandal," he said.

Two Heads in a Concrete Block

Warren Lincoln, who encased the heads of his wife and brother-in-law in a concrete block. *Beacon News Archives*.

"Besides, I needed proof; after all, having been a lawyer, I know something about the rules of evidence."

Chief Michels told him to be careful about the man he believed was watching him and suggested that Warren get a gun. Lincoln replied that he had a pistol but that it was old and rusty and probably wouldn't work. He said he would buy a new one, and Michels promised to assign an officer to keep an eye on the Lincoln house. Nothing further developed for several months.

Early in April, Lincoln returned to the police station and reported to Chief Michels that he had not seen the stranger in some time. Apparently, he had been scared off—or called off—the job. However, he did have something that he wanted the police chief to see. He unfolded two personal ads that had been clipped from the classified advertising columns of a Chicago newspaper. One of them read:

George J.—I am in Seattle. Quit W.L. for keeps. Come. Lina

George J., Lincoln explained, was a man who lived in Mt. Pulaski, Illinois, and had once kept company with Lina. Some of the arguments between Warren and his wife had been over the fact that Lina had recently contacted this man again through the newspaper personal column and had seen him during visits to Chicago.

The other clipping read:

Ralph: Have chance to see the world.
Both have job on yacht cruising the Orient for three months. Lina

Warren told Chief Michels that his wife had another brother, Ralph, and that she often kept in touch with him through the personal columns. "As you can see from these clippings, I'm not likely to be bothered by her for at least some months to come," he told Michels.

On Sunday morning, April 29, John Lincoln arrived from Chicago for a visit with his father. Late in the afternoon, Edward joined them, and at 7:30 p.m., John said that he was going to Batavia, a few miles to the north, to see some friends. His father decided to walk with him as far as the train stop and then take in a picture show at the local theatre.

During the night, Edward saw the light burning in his brother's window, but the next morning, he noticed that no smoke was coming from his brother's chimney. Later, as he headed to the greenhouse, there was still no sign of Warren. Worried, he went to the house, and there he discovered that a bedroom window had been thrown wide open—with blood on the sill. The house had been ransacked. The covers and sheets had been pulled from Warren's bed. His clothes were thrown in a rumpled heap on a chair. A desk had been smashed open, and one of the drawers was missing. Blood spots outside the open window led to the greenhouse and to a heavy club, also bloodstained, that was on the floor. Near the club were several business cards that read, "MILO DURAND, Private Detective, Criminal Tracings a Specialty."

After the police were summoned to the house, Chief Michels and Sheriff W.E. Orr discovered the imprint of a woman's high-heeled shoe in the soft earth near the house. About one hundred yards away, they found the missing desk drawer. It contained letters from relatives, apparently written in reply to letters from Warren about his marital problems. Near the spot where the drawer had been recovered, investigators found an old cistern. A bundle floating in the water proved to be a nightshirt, in which had been wrapped a nightcap and a woman's tan glove.

The police were now searching for a body. They drained the cistern, which turned out to be empty, and sifted through the ashes in the large furnace in the greenhouse. They found nothing more suspicious than a few pieces of charred metal. They also dug through a field behind the house, with no results.

Six weeks passed, and Warren Lincoln was widely assumed to be dead. Then, suddenly, he turned up back in Aurora. He had been kidnapped, he told startled police officers, by his wife and her brother. His story went that he had returned home on the night of April 29 to find Byron and Lina waiting for him. They demanded certain letters and papers, but Warren insisted they were not in the house. Finally, he was beaten into unconsciousness, and when he awoke, he was in a car. "They drove me to Cleveland, and delivered me into the hands of a dope gang to which they belonged. I escaped as soon as I could, but for a long time, feared to show myself here. I was afraid they would come back for me," he told Chief Michels.

Warren was shaken and distraught by his ordeal, and he told the chief that he planned to check himself into a sanitarium in Michigan to rest his nerves. He departed a few days later and, this time, did not return until the fall. He stayed in Aurora for a few days and then left town once again.

Meanwhile, Chief Michels was launching a quiet investigation into the puzzling mess. With the help of Chicago authorities, he made a number of interesting—and disturbing—discoveries. Here's what he found out:

The copy for the two personal advertisements had been written on a typewriter with a green ribbon and had been mailed to the newspaper in an envelope containing one of the "Milo Durand" business cards.

The personals had been published several weeks before Lincoln showed them to Chief Michels.

Lincoln had sent clippings of these same personals to a friend in Chicago, along with a letter written on a typewriter with a green ribbon.

Relatives of Lina's, who lived in Mt. Pulaski, had received a letter from her, signed with her name, asking that money be sent to her. The letter had been typed in green.

A man fitting the description of Warren Lincoln had, soon after Warren's purported abduction, cashed a check made out to Byron Shoup at a bank in Evanston. The check had been made out as payable to the bearer, but the date showed signs of alteration.

A man resembling Warren Lincoln had ordered the "Milo Durand" business cards at a printing shop in a small town outside of Chicago.

At the time that Lincoln told Chief Michels that he owned only an old and rusted revolver, he had in his possession a second gun, which Marie Klein had seen in the house when she first went to work there.

Analysis of the stains on the windowsill, and on some of Warren's clothing found after his disappearance, showed that the blood came from a chicken.

Early in January 1924, a year after Lina and her brother "departed" from Aurora, Chief Michels made a trip to Chicago. When he returned, he took Warren Lincoln into custody. In the interrogation room, he detailed the various discoveries that he had made and asked Lincoln to explain them. Warren said that he could not. At that, the chief demanded to know what had become of Lincoln's wife and brother-in-law.

Lincoln laughed and told him that he would find no bodies in this particular case—no bodies, therefore no case and no conviction. He offered to tell Chief Michels what had become of Lina and Byron but insisted that he would never tell his story to a judge and a jury.

He recounted that, one year earlier, at a time when his wife and brother-in-law were making his life a continual nightmare, an idea occurred to him while reading a newspaper story about Henri Landru, the so-called "French Bluebeard." Landru had killed numerous women and had disposed of them, presumably in a large stove in his home, so effectively that no trace of them was ever recovered. Lincoln wondered what Landru had done with the women's heads but then thought of a story that he had once read about a murderous sculptor who had concealed the body of his victim in a plaster cast and stood it among the pieces on display in his studio.

On the night of January 10, 1923, Lincoln shot Byron and Lina, and over the course of the next several nights, having told his brother that the pair had left town, he cremated their dismembered bodies in the greenhouse furnace. He sifted the ashes, retrieved buttons and other articles that had not been completely consumed and then dumped the evidence in the nearby Fox River.

The only thing left had been their heads. He placed them in a large wooden flower box and then covered them with quicklime. He shoveled a deep layer of soil over the lime and placed a plant in it. He then placed the box in the greenhouse and watered it every day. When warm weather arrived, he moved the box and plant to his front porch, where he often sat with his feet propped up on the box, chatting with friends and neighbors who stopped by. None of them had any idea of what grisly horrors the box held!

Soon, Warren had another idea. He encased the box in concrete so that it looked like a solid block. He used the block to support one end of his sagging front porch.

Later that spring, planning to start a new life in Chicago, he staged what he hoped would be considered his murder by the two people he had killed. Four chickens supplied the blood that he splashed around, and he used one of Lina's old shoes to make the impression in the ground that had been found outside his window. Lincoln slipped away but found himself worried and unhappy. He kept thinking about his secret flower box. What if the concrete casing should collapse under the weight of the porch? He came back to Aurora, inventing the story of his kidnapping, and removed the box and carried it to a garbage pile several hundred yards from the house.

Months later, he told Michels, he again became worried when he remembered that he had left behind the newspaper clipping about Landru. It was to retrieve this item that he had returned briefly in the fall of 1923. Lincoln stated that he knew he should have stayed away and left well enough alone. However, he was concerned that some of the Shoups' relatives might get suspicious, so he wanted to make it look as though they were alive and he was dead.

He laughed aloud once more.

But, anyway, I know I can't be convicted. The quicklime has done its work long since. Neither Byron nor Lina had any dental work by which the heads could be identified. The skulls might belong to any man or woman. I alone know their identities, and I'm not going to tell—not in court!

Warren Lincoln proudly and confidently showed Michels where he had concealed the concrete box, and soon after, its contents became important exhibits in a murder trial that turned out to be a humiliating disappointment to the killer. He had made one stupendous error in his attempt at a perfect crime.

There had been two barrels of quicklime in the greenhouse. One had contained harmless slaked lime and the other had been filled with unslaked, caustic quicklime, which would have easily disposed of any body part that had been sealed in it. Unfortunately for Warren Lincoln, one of his hired men had accidentally switched the labels on the two barrels, and unknowingly, Warren had dipped into the wrong barrel and had preserved the two human heads instead of destroying them. It proved to be a fatal mistake.

Thanks largely to an insanity defense, Lincoln won a verdict of life imprisonment for his crimes. He died seventeen years later at the state penitentiary in Joliet.

The Starved Rock Murders

The land around legendary Starved Rock, near Utica, is a place of great history and intense tragedy. The first blood was spilled here more than three hundred years ago, and it has been the scene of death and dark deeds ever since.

Before Starved Rock gained its infamous name, the huge stone outcropping was the site of Fort St. Louis, a French sanctuary and trading post. According to legend, it gained its infamous name in the early part of the 1700s, when the Illiniwek Indians were largely wiped out by their Iroquois and Fox enemies. They sought refuge on the Illinois River at the old fort that had been built by the French but soon realized they were trapped. The Illiniweks discovered they had no way to escape from the rock. Below them, the enemy waited, and at their backs was a steep drop to the rocky banks and swirling waters of the Illinois River. The Illiniwek numbers began to slowly dwindle from sickness, cold and, most of all, hunger. Most of those who tried to escape were killed after jumping from the edge of the cliff.

No one really knows how long the Illiniweks were trapped on the summit that came to be known as Starved Rock. A number of accounts say that at least a dozen of them escaped through the woods or by the river. They took shelter with friendly tribes or with French trappers. Others told stories of miraculous escapes and of a mysterious snow that fell one night and covered the tracks of the desperate Illiniweks, giving them just enough time to escape. When they were gone, they left nothing behind at the old fort save for items they could not carry and the bodies of the dead.

By the end of the ordeal, the once-great Illiniwek confederation had collapsed to fewer than one hundred persons. Eventually, they were all sent to a reservation in Kansas. It is believed that not a single descendant of the Illiniwek nation still lives today. They were completely wiped out by the events at Starved Rock, and it seems that once this region got a taste for blood, it would desire it again in the years to come.

In March 1960, the violence of the past returned to Starved Rock with the discovery of the bludgeoned bodies of three women from Riverside, Illinois. The land around LaSalle's fortress had been turned into a state park years before, and on March 14, the women's bloody corpses were found in one of the park's fabulous box canyons.

The three middle-aged women—Mildred Lindquist, Lillian Oetting and Frances Murphy—had driven from their upscale homes in Riverside for a four-day holiday at Starved Rock Park. The three friends, who all attended the Riverside Presbyterian Church, had been anxious for an outing together. Oetting, who had spent the entire winter nursing her husband after a heart attack, was especially looking forward to several days of hiking, bird watching and spending time outdoors. Employees at the park's lodge would later remember the arrival of the three ladies. Frances Murphy had parked her gray station wagon in the inn's parking area, and she and her friends had unloaded their few pieces of luggage. They registered for two rooms, dropped off their bags and then ate lunch in the dining room. Afterward, they remarked to one of the staff members that it was a beautiful day for a hike, and they left carrying a camera and a small pair of binoculars.

The women walked away from the lodge wearing rubber galoshes. The path was covered with a light snow, and they trudged and slipped along, pausing occasionally to take photographs of one another. Eventually, they came to the dead end of the St. Louis Canyon, where steep, rocky walls framed a majestic frozen waterfall. The three women were only one mile from the lodge. Lillian Oetting struggled with the controls of her friend's camera and snapped several color slides of the canyon. When she was finished, the group turned to leave—and they walked into a horror that stunned the entire nation.

The first sign that something was wrong occurred that evening when George Oetting tried to telephone his wife at the lodge. She had promised to call him, but when she had not, Oetting placed his own call. He was told by staff on duty at the desk that his wife was not available. It was surmised that the ladies had gone out somewhere, and the staff member suggested

The frozen waterfall at the dead end of Starved Rock's St. Louis Canyon. Although this is a recent photograph, it looks much the same as it would have in 1960, when the murders occurred.

that Oetting would call her husband in the morning. Unconcerned, George Oetting went to bed.

On Tuesday morning, he called the lodge again and, once more, asked to speak to his wife. The employee who answered mistakenly told the worried man that the three women had been seen at breakfast and were simply out of the lodge at that time. Reassured, Oetting ended the call.

That night, a late winter storm hit the Illinois Valley. In the St. Louis Canyon, several inches of snow covered up footprints, bloodstains and other vital pieces of information around three cold and still bodies. The near-blizzard conditions continued all night long, making the roads in the park nearly impassable.

George Oetting telephoned the lodge again on Wednesday morning, but his wife and her friends could still not be located. At his insistence, employees entered the women's rooms and found that the beds and bags were untouched. A quick check of the parking lot also showed that the Murphy station wagon had not been moved. Shocked, Oetting realized that his wife and her friends had now been missing for more than forty hours.

As soon as Oetting broke off the call, he telephoned his longtime friend, Virgil W. Peterson, the operating director of the Chicago Crime Commission. When Peterson learned of the news, he contacted the state police and other law enforcement agencies in the area. Within minutes, word of the missing women had reached the LaSalle County sheriff's office, and Sheriff Ray Eutsey began organizing search parties to look for the women. He accompanied one of the groups that left immediately for the park.

Bill Danley, a local newspaper reporter, was just finishing his last story for the day's edition when he got a tip about the disappearances. Grabbing a camera, he braved the snow-packed roads and headed for the park. When Danley reached the park's west entrance, he noticed a boy running across an icy ravine toward the road. He drove to a small parking area and found several other youths shouting that bodies had been found on one of the trails. Danley recognized the boys as members of the nearby Illinois Youth Commission Forestry Camp, where he had once led an Explorer Post, and he pulled them aside to a nearby storage garage for some questions. When they told him of the bodies, he called the lodge, where law enforcement officials had gathered, and then called the newspaper to report the discovery. In a matter of minutes, the story was flashing across news wires around the country.

Danley was among those who entered the St. Louis Canyon and got the first look at the bodies. The three mutilated women were lying side by side, partially covered with snow. They were on their backs, under a small ledge; their lower clothing had been torn away, and their legs were spread open. Each of them had been beaten viciously about the head, and two of the bodies were tied together with heavy white twine. They were covered with blood, and their exposed legs were blackened with bruises.

State police detectives soon arrived and began a search of the immediate area. Except for the floor of the overhang where the bodies were found, the entire canyon was covered in nearly six inches of snow. The fine, white powder had to be carefully removed, and as it was, signs of a violent struggle were revealed. Mrs. Murphy's camera was found about ten feet from the victims. Its leather case was smeared with blood, and its strap was broken. Searchers also found the women's bloody binoculars. A short distance away, LaSalle County's state's attorney Harland Warren stumbled across a frozen tree limb that was streaked with blood. The snow beneath it was covered with blood, and it was realized that this was likely the murder weapon. A trail of gore also led police to speculate that the women had been killed deeper in the canyon and then their bodies had been dragged and positioned under the rock ledge. The bodies remained in place for hours, until pathologists and state crime lab officials could arrive. The vigil lasted long into the night, and then, aided by lanterns and flashlights, the victims were removed on cloth stretchers.

The bodies were taken to the Hulse Funeral Home in Ottawa, where they were examined and autopsied. The women had obviously been molested, but the cold, and limitations of medical techniques at the time, failed to find any evidence of rape. The doctors were able to determine the time of death, placing it shortly after they had enjoyed lunch at the lodge. No motive was suggested for the murders, but robbery was dismissed, as the women had left their money and jewelry behind in their rooms when they went for their afternoon hike.

The investigation went nowhere almost from the start. There were few clues to follow, and theories began to grow wilder and wilder. Things were further confused by all of those who wanted to maintain jurisdiction in the case. State's Attorney Warren, a hardworking and respected official, was technically in charge, but the state police maintained their authority in the case because the murders were committed on park property. The two law enforcement camps clashed, but Warren was in a bind. He was forced to deal with the state authorities because the officials in LaSalle County simply had no experience dealing with crimes of this manner.

As the investigation slowly moved forward, fear was gripping the region. Doors that were never locked before were now firmly secured. Hardware stores experienced a run on new deadbolts, and sporting goods stores saw guns vanish from their cases at an alarming rate. The number of overnight guests at the Starved Rock Lodge dropped off to almost nothing, and some motorists went miles out of their way to avoid driving near the canyon entrance. Newspapers and radio broadcasters around the state widely reported the slow progress of the investigation and elevated the level of panic in the area.

The continued newspaper scrutiny of the case kept pressure on police officials to make progress, especially at Harland Warren's county office. He was doing everything in his power to move the investigation forward, but he had a hard time coping with the pressure, especially during an election year. Money was becoming a problem as well, since the investigation budget was soaring. Throughout 1960, he was under ever-increasing pressure to solve the murders. Frustrated, he felt that he had taken enough criticism for the investigation. He was an attorney, not a detective, but he decided to take one last desperate run at the case. He asked himself what the killer had left behind at the scene of the crime, and the obvious answer was the twine that he had used to bind two of the victims.

Using his own money, Warren purchased a microscope and began intently conducting a study of the twine. Research revealed that there were two kinds of twine used, a twenty-ply cord and a twelve-ply one. With this information in hand, he sought out help to follow the lead. Instead of choosing someone from his staff, he handpicked two county detectives who would report to him alone. The two men were deputies Bill Dummett and Wayne Hess. They were both trustworthy and intelligent and would not leak the details of what Warren was doing to the newspapers.

The men chose the most logical place to start the search for the source of the twine: Starved Rock Lodge. In September 1960, Warren and his deputies met with the manager of the lodge's kitchen. Within minutes, and without much difficulty, Warren found both kinds of twine used in the murder. They were each used for wrapping food, and Dummett and Hess, using lodge purchasing records, soon tracked down the twine's manufacturer. The twine used to bind the murder victims had been taken, without question, from the supply in the lodge's kitchen. Just as Warren had always suspected, the killer either worked at, or had access to, the park's lodge.

Faced with the fact that all of the lodge employees had been given polygraph tests, and had passed, Warren now had to wonder if the tests had been accurate. He boldly decided that it was time to run some of his own tests. Hiring a specialist from a prominent Chicago firm, Warren re-called all of the employees who had worked during the week of the murder. One by one, they came to a small cabin located near the lodge and again submitted to an exam. The first dozen or so were quickly cleared, and Warren and the deputies wondered if they might be wasting their time. Then Bill Dummett brought in a former dishwasher named Chester Otto Weger, and everything changed.

When Weger's polygraph test was completed, Warren noticed that the examiner's face had gone pale. As soon as Weger left the cabin, the technician ended months of endless leads and wasted time. He turned to Warren and the two deputies and quietly stated, "That's your man."

Weger, twenty-one, was a slight, small man with a wife and two young children. He had worked at the park until that summer, when he resigned to go into business with his father as a house painter. Dummett remembered the man's name from an earlier police report, but he had never made much of an impression on the investigators. Warren intensified the investigation of the man, and strangely, Weger happily cooperated with him. He surrendered a piece of a buckskin jacket that he owned so that some suspicious "dark stains" on it could be examined. It later turned out to be human blood, but in 1960, it could not be typed and matched to a specific victim. Warren also asked Weger to submit to further polygraph tests, and again, Weger agreed. He was given an entire series of tests, and he failed all of them.

Once the jacket was determined to be stained with blood, Warren put the former dishwasher under constant surveillance by the state police. Warren, along with Dummett and Weger, began checking into Weger's past and also into similar crimes in the area that might have escalated into murder. Dummett came across a reported rape and robbery that took place about a mile from Starved Rock in 1959. With Warren's approval, he approached the young female victim with a stack of mug shots. As she slowly sorted through them, she began to scream as she came across the face of Chester Weger.

With this positive identification, Warren could have easily ordered Weger arrested, but he was forced to wait. A new problem had reared its ugly head. With all of the time and energy involved in the investigation, Warren had worked very little on his campaign for reelection. If he booked Weger on rape and murder charges before the election, defense attorneys would simply say that he had done so as a stunt to retain his job. He left Weger under surveillance, not wanting to jeopardize the case against him with the election. Confident of his record of cleaning gambling and prostitution out of LaSalle County during his eight years in office, Warren let his past actions speak for themselves. Unfortunately, his opponent let the "bungling" of the Starved Rock murder case speak for him. Out of sixty thousand votes case in the election, Warren lost by nearly thirty-five hundred.

Disappointed by the election results, Warren still had time in office to pursue the case against Weger. Although his evidence was not as strong as he would have liked, he obtained an arrest warrant against Weger for the 1959 rape and ordered Hess and Dummett to pick him up. Warren believed that when he saw all of the evidence mounting against him, Weger would confess to the crime—and to the Starved Rock murders.

Warren made careful plans with his two deputies about how to interrogate Weger before confronting him with murder charges. A short time later, Hess and Dummett arrived at the young man's apartment and explained that they had some more questions for him. They made no mention of the arrest warrants that were waiting at the courthouse. Once they had him in custody, the officers began to question him about the rape and also began to press him about the murders. They kept him in the interrogation room until past midnight, and then finally, weary of questions and nearly exhausted, Weger stopped in midsentence and asked to see his family. A police car was dispatched to his parents' home in Oglesby, and his mother and father were brought to the courthouse. Dummett and Hess gave them a few minutes alone with their son.

In his official statement, which was taken the next day, Deputy Hess stated:

> *When Bill stepped out of the back room in the states attorney's office to show Mr. and Mrs. Weger to the door so they could go home, I could see that something was bothering Chester. I said "Chester, why don't you tell me about it? There are just the two of us here…just tell me about it." He said, "All right. I did it. I got scared. I tried to grab their pocketbook, they fought and I hit them." The pocketbook that Weger claimed that he tried to take was actually Mrs. Murphy's camera.*

Minutes later, the confession was transcribed and signed by Weger. During the confession, when he was asked why he had dragged the bodies under the overhang in the St. Louis Canyon, Weger said that he had spotted a small airplane flying low over the park. Weger said that he was afraid that it was a state police plane, so he moved the bodies so that they could not be seen from above. A few days later, the flight over the park was confirmed by the pilot's testimony and logbook.

Weger confessed several more times to the murders over the next few days and even reenacted the killings for a crowd of policemen and reporters at the canyon. Then, suddenly, after his first meeting with his court-appointed attorney, Weger changed his story and stated that he was innocent of all of the charges. Weger claimed that Dummett and Hess had coerced a confession from him by threatening him with a gun. He had lied in his confession but had been so scared that he signed the papers anyway. Weger also said that Dummett had fed him the information about the airplane. He claimed to be in Oglesby at the time of the killings.

Weger was brought to trial. Jury selection took almost two weeks, and the trial began on January 20, 1961. The new state's attorney, Robert E. Richardson, was in charge of the prosecution and was assisted by Anthony Raccuglia. The trial, which gained national attention, was presided over by Judge Leonard Hoffman, and because the two prosecutors had never tried a murder case before, he suggested that Harland Warren be named as a special prosecutor

Chester Otto Weger at his trial. *Illinois State Historical Library*.

for this case only. Richardson, who had strongly criticized Warren during the election, dismissed the idea. Richardson and Raccuglia decided to file charges against Weger for only one of the three murders. The reason for this was that, in the event of a mistrial or an acquittal, they could still file charges against him for the other killings. They sought the death penalty in the case.

On March 4, almost exactly a year after the murders, the jury brought back a guilty verdict for Chester Weger. On the day of his twenty-second birthday, he was sentenced to a term of life imprisonment. After Judge Hoffman dismissed the jurors, reporters asked them if they knew that a life sentence in Illinois meant that Weger would be eligible for parole in a few years. Most of the jurors were shocked—they had no idea. Some of them even said that if they had known that Weger was not really being sent away for the rest of his life, they would have voted for the electric chair. A lack of knowledge of Illinois law, and the prosecutor's failure to properly instruct the jury, ended up saving Weger's life.

Chester Weger was incarcerated at the Statesville Penitentiary in Joliet and remains in prison today at the Illinois River Correctional Center in Canton. Weger has been denied parole two dozen times since 1972, and most feel that he belongs securely behind bars.

However, in the minds of some people, there are questions about the case that remain unanswered. Many feel that the evidence that was used to convict Weger would not stand up in court today. His prosecution largely turned out to be based on his confession, which predated Miranda warnings that are required today. Others question how a small, slight man like Weger could have overpowered three middle-aged women and then move their bodies by himself to leave them hidden under the rocky overhang.

Others who believe in Weger's innocence point to a "deathbed confession" that allegedly occurred in 1982 or 1983. A Chicago police sergeant named Mark Gibson submitted an affidavit in 2006 that recounted the confession. It was being used in court to support a motion for new DNA tests in the Starved Rock murder case. In the affidavit, Gibson stated that he and his partner, now deceased, were called to Rush–St. Luke's Presbyterian Hospital to see a terminally ill patient who wanted to "clear her conscience."

The affidavit stated, "The woman was lying in a hospital bed. I went over toward her, and she grabbed hold of my hand. She indicated that when she was younger, she had been with her friends at a state park when something happened."

The woman then told Gibson that she was at a park in Utica, and things "got out of hand," multiple victims were killed and "they dragged the bodies."

Gibson said that the woman's daughters cut the interview short, shouting that their mother was "out of her mind" and ordering the police from the room. In the affidavit, Gibson did not provide the exact date of the interview, or the woman's name, but said he passed the information along to a detective. The affidavit did not address whether there was any follow-up or why the confession was not presented until 2006. The alleged "confession" was not allowed into the court hearings, although new DNA tests were ordered. However, they failed to clear Weger of anything because the samples had been corrupted over the years.

After these attempts for release failed, a clemency petition was sent to Governor Rod Blagojevich, but it was denied in June 2007.

To this day, Chester Weger continues to maintain that he was framed for the murders by Deputies Dummett and Hess. But both of the deputies, until the day each of them died, insisted that Weger had confessed. They firmly believed that he had committed the murders and had been the perpetrator of one of the most heinous acts in the already-bloody history of Starved Rock.

Behind the Walls of Joliet Penitentiary

For more than forty years, from Illinois' statehood in 1818 to about 1858, there was only one state penitentiary in Illinois, located in the Mississippi River town of Alton. The prison was completed in 1833 but soon deteriorated beyond repair—a major concern since the state's population—and along with it, the crime rate—was growing rapidly. During his inaugural speech in 1853, newly elected governor Joel Mattson, a Joliet native, spoke out for the need of a prison in Northern Illinois. By the mid-1800s, the population center of the state had shifted from southwestern Illinois toward the expanding city of Chicago. In 1857, spurred by scandals involving the horrific conditions of the Alton prison, the Illinois legislature finally approved a commission to scout for locations for the new penitentiary.

Governor Mattson's friend Nelson Elwood, a former mayor of Joliet, was appointed to the board of penitentiary commissioners, and it was Elwood who convinced the members of the board to build a prison at a site that was then two miles north of the city of Joliet. The location boasted a freshwater spring and proximity to railroads, the Illinois & Michigan Canal and the city of Chicago. But the greatest argument in favor of the site was the limestone deposits situated under the fifteen-acre location. The deposits were so deep that no inmate could escape by tunneling through them.

The penitentiary was designed by William Boyington in a style known as castellated Gothic. Boyington had also designed several Chicago landmarks, including the Chicago Pumping Station and the Water Tower on Michigan Avenue. The structures were all of similar style and reminiscent of medieval construction, evoking castles and, of course, dungeons. The walls of the

A historical view of the Joliet State Penitentiary. *Chicago Daily News.*

prison would be twenty-five feet high, six feet wide at the base and two feet wide at the top. Turreted guard towers anchored each corner of the site. The cellblocks were to be constructed inside long row houses, holding one hundred cells in each one.

Construction on the penitentiary began in 1858. The workforce consisted of fifty-three prisoners who had been transferred in from Alton. They lived in makeshift barracks while they mined the Joliet-Lemont limestone quarry, located just across the road from the building site. Local private contractors supervised the construction and the prisoners. Quarry drilling was done entirely by hand, and the huge blocks were hauled by mule cart to the road. A conveyor belt was later built to transport rocks to the surface. As work progressed, more prisoners were transferred to Joliet and assigned to work on the construction. There was no shortage of stone or labor, and in 1859, the first building was completed. It eventually took just twelve years for the prisoners to construct their own place of confinement. By then, the Alton prison had been completely shut down, and all of the state prisoners had been sent to Joliet.

The Joliet Penitentiary contained eleven hundred cells: nine hundred for the general population, one hundred for solitary confinement and one hundred to house female inmates. At the time it was finished, it was the largest prison in the United States and was adopted as an architectural model for penitentiaries around the world, including Leavenworth and the Isle of Pines in Cuba.

Prisoners were housed in two-man cells that were six by nine feet, with no electricity, plumbing or running water. Each cell had a pitcher for fresh water and a bucket for waste. The stone walls of the cells were eight inches thick, with only the door and a small ventilation hole for openings. The cellblocks were built running the length of the middle of the long row house, away from any natural light. The cells were grim, confined, dimly lighted chambers that offered little hope for the men (and women) incarcerated in them.

Life in the new penitentiary was harsh and sometimes brutal. The plan for the Joliet prison was based on the dreaded Auburn System, which was created in Auburn, New York, in the early 1800s. The inmates at Joliet passed their days under a strict regime of silence but were allowed to speak to their cellmates during the evening hours in quiet voices. Contact with the outside world was severely limited, and no recreational activities were offered.

Prisoners moved from place to place within the prison using a lock step formation, a sort of side step shuffle with one hand on the shoulder of the man in front. Inmates' heads had to be turned in the direction of the guards, who watched for any lip movement that signaled when someone was talking. The lock step formation also made it easier for one guard to watch over a larger number of prisoners. Floggings, stocks and extensive time in solitary confinement were common punishments for those who broke the rules. The inmates wore striped uniforms all year round. Men who were deemed to be escape risks were shackled in irons.

Convict labor, under constant discipline, allowed the Joliet Penitentiary to initiate factory-style working conditions at a profit. Lucrative contracts were sold to the highest private bidder, who then sold the products manufactured in the prison on the open market. Under the constant scrutiny of the guards, the prisoners were put to work producing an array of goods: rattan furniture, shoes, brooms, chairs, wheelbarrows, horse collars and dressed limestone. The prison was also self-sufficient in most aspects of daily life. It had a thriving bakery, a tailor shop, a hospital and a library, which was administered by the prison chaplain.

A prisoner's day began at 6:00 a.m., when he was marched into the prison yard to empty his waste bucket into the sewage ditch. He then marched into the kitchen and back to his cell for a breakfast of hash, bread and coffee. When the dining hall was completed in 1907, prisoners were allowed to eat communally but in silence. Prisoners in solitary confinement received a daily ration of two ounces of bread and water.

The prison buildings were impossible to keep warm in the winter and very hard to keep clean, making them a breeding ground for lice, rats and various diseases. Tuberculosis, pneumonia and typhoid were the main causes of death among inmates. Unclaimed bodies were buried in a pauper's graveyard, called Monkey Hill, near the prison on Woodruff Street.

The strict silence, unsanitary conditions, forced labor and harsh punishments gave the Joliet Penitentiary a reputation as the last possible place that a man wanted to end up.

Prison reform was first introduced at Joliet in 1913 with the appointment of Edmund Allen as the warden. By 1915, the striped uniforms and the lock step formation were gone and the rule of silence ended. Prisoners were allowed recreation privileges, and a baseball diamond was built. Warden Allen also started an honor farm on twenty-two hundred acres of land four miles north of the prison. Prisoners were allowed to work in the fields, and on the farm, as a reward for good conduct.

Ironically, though, Warden Allen, who lived in an apartment on the prison grounds with his wife, Odette, experienced personal tragedy, possibly at the

Reform warden Edmund Allen. *Chicago Daily News.*

The room where Odette Allen, the warden's wife, was killed in 1915, murdered by one of the inmates whom Allen's reforms tried to help. *Chicago Daily News.*

hands of one of the trusted inmates. On June 19, 1915, Warden Allen and his wife planned to leave on a trip to West Baden, Indiana. Mrs. Allen's dressmaker had not quite finished two of her dresses, and Odette persuaded her husband to go ahead and leave without her. Early the next morning, a fire broke out in the warden's apartment. When the prison fire department responded, they discovered Mrs. Allen dead and her bed engulfed in flames. The fire was ruled as arson, and trusty "Chicken Joe" Campbell, who had been Mrs. Allen's servant, was charged with the crime. Campbell was tried, convicted and sentenced to death, despite the fact that the evidence against him was purely circumstantial. At Warden Allen's request, Governor Dunne commuted his sentenced to life imprisonment.

Construction on a new prison, called Stateville, began in 1916 on the land where the honor farm was located. It was originally intended to replace the older prison, but the national crime sprees of the 1920s and 1930s kept the old Joliet Penitentiary open for more than eighty years.

During its time in operation, the prison housed some of the most infamous and deadly criminals in Illinois history. Some of them were already well known when they walked through the front gates, but others gained their infamy inside the walls.

The first execution at the prison took place during the Civil War years, in the spring of 1864. George Chase, a convicted horse thief, attempted to escape from the penitentiary. When he was confronted by Deputy Warden

Joseph Clark, Chase attacked Clark with a club and hit him so hard in the head that he killed the officer. Chase was recaptured, charged with murder and sentenced to hang—turning a short sentence for stealing horses into the death penalty. Chase was hanged a short time later and became the first inmate to be executed at Joliet.

Famous Chicago gangster George "Bugs" Moran served three terms for robbery at Joliet between 1910 and 1923. After the murder of his crime mentor Dion O'Banion in 1926, Moran became the leader of Chicago's North Side bootleggers. His time in power lasted until 1929, when seven of his men were slaughtered by the Capone Gang in the St. Valentine's Day Massacre. Moran turned to a life of petty crime and died in Leavenworth in 1957.

Frank McErlane was considered one of the most vicious gunmen in Chicago and, before being sent to Joliet, was credited with killing nine men, two women and a dog. Arrested for his part in the murder of an Oak Park police officer in 1916, he served one year at Joliet before trying to escape. He was caught and served another two years for the attempt. Shortly after the start of Prohibition, McErlane began running a gang with partner Joseph "Polack Joe" Saltis on Chicago's South Side. Later, they allied with the Capone Gang against the West Side O'Donnell Brothers. During the war with the O'Donnells, McErlane introduced the Thompson machine gun to Chicago and, with it, killed at least fifteen men during the Beer Wars. McErlane was suspected to have taken part in the St. Valentine's Day Massacre, and he suffered serious wounds during a gun battle with George Moran in 1930. While McErlane was recovering, Moran sent two gunmen to kill him, but McErlane pulled a revolver from underneath his pillow and began firing, driving off the surprised gangsters. McErlane was wounded in the gunfight, suffering two wounds in his injured leg and one in his arm, but he recovered. In 1932, he became ill with pneumonia and died within days.

Nathan Leopold and Richard Loeb, two college students from wealthy families, were sentenced to life imprisonment at Joliet in 1924 after kidnapping and murdering fourteen-year-old Bobby Franks. They had been attempting to pull off the "perfect crime." Warden John L. Whitman was firm in his assertion that the young men received the same treatment as the other prisoners, but his claims were nowhere near the truth. Leopold and Loeb lived in luxury compared to the rest of the inmates. Each enjoyed a private cell, books, a desk, a filing cabinet and even pet birds. They also showered away from the other prisoners and took their meals, which were prepared to order, in the officers' lounge. Leopold was allowed to keep a flower garden. They were also permitted any number of unsupervised visitors and were allowed to keep their own gardens. The doors to their cells were usually left open, and they had passes to visit one another at any time. Loeb was stabbed to death by another inmate in 1936. Leopold was eventually released in 1958, after pleas to the prison board by poet Carl Sandburg. He moved to Puerto Rico and died in 1971.

George "Baby Face" Nelson also served time at Joliet. In July 1931, he was convicted of robbing the Itasca State Bank and sentenced to one year to life at Joliet Penitentiary. He served two months before being sent to stand trial for another bank robbery. He was under armed guard and on his way back to Joliet when he escaped and went back to robbing banks with the Dillinger Gang.

Another famous inmate was Daniel L. McGeoghagen, a racketeer, Prohibition beer maker and skilled safecracker. The McGeoghagen Gang attempted to loot three hundred safe deposit boxes in 1947, but when things went wrong, they ended up taking seven people hostage. A gun battle with the police ensued, leaving two people dead and two wounded. McGeoghagen was captured, tried and sentenced to twenty years at Joliet. He was paroled in 1958.

One of the more recent inmates at Joliet was serial killer John Wayne Gacy, one of Chicago's most notorious murderers. Between 1972 and 1978, Gacy tortured and killed thirty-three young men, burying twenty-eight of them under his home. He was sentenced to death in 1980 and spent some of his time on death row in a cell at the Joliet Penitentiary.

The 1970s saw the rise of gang violence within the penitentiary's walls. The Gangster Disciples, the Vice Lords, the Latin Kings and the P. Stone Nation all vied for power, leading to a riot in April 1975. A group of two hundred P. Stone Nation gang members took twelve prison workers hostage and held a cellblock for five hours. Herbert Catlett, a former member of the gang, attempted to intervene on behalf of the hostages. He was serving time for armed robbery and trying to turn his life around for when he was released. When the hostages were eventually set free, Catlett was found with his throat slashed.

In 2001, the Joliet State Penitentiary was closed down. The crumbling old prison had finally been deemed unfit for habitation, and all of the prisoners were moved out. Today, the Joliet Penitentiary still stands, slowly crumbling as the years pass by. What will become of this old place? Many locals consider it an eyesore and embarrassment, but still others see it as an important place in Illinois history. It has been a target for the wrecking ball and has been named as a possible historic site, but for now, its future remains uncertain.

Bibliography

Angle, Paul. *Bloody Williamson*. New York: Alfred A. Knopf, 1952.

Brannon, W.T. "Album of Famous Mysteries." Syndicated newspaper column, 1940s–1950s.

Chicago Historical Society

Chicago Public Library

Churney, Dan. *Capone's Cornfields*. Charleston, SC: Booksurge, LLC, 2003.

DeNeal, Gary. *Knight of Another Sort*. Carbondale: Southern Illinois University Press, 1998.

Dickensen, Fred. "Album of Famous Mysteries." Syndicated newspaper column, 1940s–1950s.

Erickson, Gladys. *Warden Ragen of Joliet*. New York: E.R. Dutton, 1957.

Fliege, Stu. *Tales & Trails of Illinois*. Urbana: University of Illinois Press, 2002.

Howard, Robert. *Illinois: A History of the Prairie State*. Grand Rapids, MI: Erdmans, 1972.

Hynd, Alan. *Murder, Mayhem & Mystery*. New York: A.S. Barnes & Co., 1958.

Levins, Peter. "Album of Famous Mysteries." Syndicated newspaper column, 1940s–1950s.

Lewis, Lloyd. *Myths After Lincoln*. New York: Harcourt, Brace & Co, 1929.

Nash, Jay Robert. *Bloodletters and Bad Men*. New York: M. Evans and Company, Inc., 1995.

Parrish, Randall. *Historic Illinois*. Chicago: A.C. McClurg & Co., 1905.

Pensoneau, Taylor. *Brothers Notorious*. New Berlin, IL: Downstate Publications, 2002.

Quaife, Milo. *Chicago Highways Old and New*. Chicago: D.F. Keller & Co., 1923.

Sifakis, Carl. *Encyclopedia of American Crime*. New York: Facts on File, 1982.

Speer, Bonnie Stahlman. *The Great Abraham Lincoln Hijack*. Norman, OK: Reliance Press, 1990.

Taylor, Troy. *Bloody Illinois*. Decatur, IL: Whitechapel Press, 2008.

———. *Dead Men Do Tell Tales*. Decatur, IL: Whitechapel Press, 2008.

———. *True Crime: Illinois*. Mechanicsburg, PA: Stackpole Books, 2009.

Waugh, Daniel. *Egan's Rats*. Nashville, TN: Cumberland House, 2007.

MAGAZINES, NEWSPAPERS AND PERIODICALS

Chicago American
Chicago Daily News
Decatur Daily Review
Chicago Daily Tribune
Chicago Herald & Examiner
Chicago Sun-Times
Front Page Detective Magazine
Jacksonville Journal-Courier
New York Times
Peoria Journal-Star
Peoria Times-Observer
Rockford Register-Star
Springfield State Journal-Register
St. Louis Post-Dispatch
True Magazine

About the Author

Troy Taylor is an occultist, supernatural historian and the author of seventy-five books on ghosts, hauntings, history, crime and the unexplained in America. He is also the founder of the American Ghost Society and the owner of the Illinois and American Hauntings Tour companies.

Taylor shares a birthday with one of his favorite authors, F. Scott Fitzgerald, but instead of living in New York and Paris like Fitzgerald, Taylor grew up in Illinois. Raised on the prairies of the state, he developed an interest in "things that go bump in the night" at an early age. As a young man, he channeled that interest into developing ghost tours and writing about haunts in Chicago and Central Illinois.

Troy and his wife, Haven, currently reside in Chicago's West Loop neighborhood.

Visit us at
www.historypress.net